Business Knowledge for IT in Prime Brokerage

A complete handbook for IT professionals

PROFESSIONAL SERIES

Essvale Corporation Limited
63 Apollo Building
1 Newton Place
London E14 3TS
www.essvale.com

This is the first edition of this publication.

All rights reserved
Copyright © Essvale Corporation Ltd, 2008

Essvale Corporation Ltd is hereby identified as author
of this work in accordance with Section 77 of the
Copyright, Designs and Patents Act 1988

Requests to the authors should be addressed to:
permissions@essvale.com.

This book is sold subject to the conditions that it shall not,
by way of trade or otherwise, be lent, resold, hired out or
otherwise circulated without the author's or publisher's prior
consent in any form of binding or cover other than that in
which it is published and without a similar condition including
this condition being imposed on the subsequent purchaser.

A CIP record for this book is available from the British Library

ISBN (10-digit) 9781906096038
ISBN (13-digit) 1906096031

This publication is designed to provide accurate and authoritative
information about the subject matter. The author makes no representation,
express or implied, with regard to the accuracy of the information
contained in the publication and cannot accept any responsibility or
liability for any errors or omissions that it may contain.

Cover design by Essvale Design Team
Design and typesetting by Boldface, London EC1
Printed by Lightning Source Ltd, Milton Keynes

Preface

Not so long ago, hedge funds were spending $10 billion on prime brokerage services, according to research sources. Record trading volumes and inflows into the alternatives space have pushed that figure even higher, and experts predict demand to continue to rise. This growth has created huge shifts in the industry, with the big names in prime brokerage – Goldman Sachs and Morgan Stanley – scrambling to maintain their place at the top. Meanwhile, other major players have been quietly restructuring their businesses and are winning an increasing share of the market by investing heavily in customer service and focusing on becoming one-stop shops for all hedge fund needs.

The business of prime brokerage is booming. For readers who are not already aware of it, prime brokerage is a special group of services that a dedicated division or arm of an investment bank gives to special clients. The fortunes of the prime brokerage industry are tied to those of the providers – the investment banks – and the beneficiaries or the benefactors (depending on the viewpoint of the reader) – the clients – that are usually hedge funds.

Despite the credit crunch in recent years, hedge funds are still poised for "supercharged" returns in the near future; in fact experts believe that hedge funds are well positioned to take advantage of the crisis, especially in the secondary loans market.

IT in prime brokerage is also set for a massive boom as investment in technology is a source of competitive advantage. Relatively new technologies such as straight-through processing (STP), direct markets access (DMA) and algorithmic trading are being embraced by both prime brokers and their hedge fund clients and this has helped push technology to the top of the agenda in the prime brokerage industry. In addition, recent initiatives in messaging protocols and derivatives processing are also allowing technology to shape the prime brokerage industry.

Technology is a key offering among the gamut of services offered by prime brokers. For instance, if a hedge fund requires an order management, electronic trading platform, real-time P&L, portfolio accounting, risk reporting, performance measurement and partnership accounting – processes driven by technology – a prime broker can provide the entire suite.

All these factors underscore the importance of technology in this sector. IT professionals need a thorough understanding of not only the business aspects of prime brokerage, but the application of technology to the prime brokerage business as it appears that their contribution is invaluable to the sustainable future of this increasingly important sector of the financial services industry.

Acknowledgements

Essvale Corporation Limited would like to thank all authors and publishers of all materials used in compiling this publication. Also thanks to all the respondents to the research carried out to justify writing this publication.

We would like to acknowledge Ann C. Logue, Cary Goldstein, David Newman and Anita Nemes of Merrill Lynch, Robert Maloney of Credit Suisse, Sameer Shalaby of Paladyne Systems, Lisa Jane O'Neil of LJO Associates, Joseph Miller of TZero, also Clare Beesley of Risk Books, Dominic Hobson of Global Custodian , Paul Dentskevich of HSH Nordbank AG, Jon Shamah of Core Street, Nick Boch of Celent, Sharon Wright, James Warfield and Rachael Sharkey of Sungard.

Our thanks also go to Pat Winfield of Bookworm Editorial Services, Barney Lodge of Lodge Consulting, Dr Moritz Hagenmüller and Sharon Ohrndorf of BOD, Boldface Typesetters, the helpful staff of City Business Library and Idea Store Canary Wharf, the editors and support staff at Nielsen Book Data, Lucy Sharp of Lightning Source, Trey Smith of Ingram Digital, Graham Morris and Vic Daniels of Hereisthecity.com, the staff of Amazon and other bookstores worldwide .Thanks for supporting Bizle Professional Series thus far.

Contents

Preface	iv
Acknowledgements	v
Contents	vii
Introduction	xi

1. Overview of Prime Brokerage — **1**

Introduction	2
Definition of Prime Brokerage	2
History of Prime Brokerage	3
Risk Management for Hedge Funds	4
Prime Brokerage Fee Structure	4
Global Prime Brokerage Market	5
List of some Prime Brokers	9

2 Overview of Hedge Funds — **11**

Introduction	12
What are Hedge Funds?	12
Definition of Hedge Funds	13
Key Characteristics of Hedge Funds	14
Reasons for Investing in Hedge Funds	15
Types of Hedge Fund Strategies	15
Fee Structure	18
World's 10 Best Hedge Funds	19
Global Hedge Fund Industry	21
Source of Investments	22

3. The Relationship between Prime Brokers and Hedge Funds — **25**

Introduction	26
Role of the Prime Broker	26
Overview of Products and Services offered by Prime Brokers	26
Risk Management for Hedge Funds	32
What Hedge Funds Want from Prime Brokers	34
Legal Aspects of the Prime Broker–Hedge Fund Relationship	37

4. The Trading and Economic Factors Driving the Relationship — **41**

Introduction	42
The "Relationship" Side of the Trading and Economic Factors	42
Differences between Prime Brokerage Services	43
Economics	44
Prime Brokerage Costs	47
Leverage	48
Intermediation	49
Conclusion	50

5. The Business Environment — 53

Introduction — 54
The Environmental Factors affecting Prime Brokers — 54
The Global Custodian Prime Brokerage Survey — 58
Allied Industries — 59
Security Identifier Types — 66

6. Trends in Prime Brokerage — 69

Introduction — 70
The Rising Importance of Prime Brokerage as a Banking Business Line — 70
Increasing Demand for Prime Brokerage Services in Credit
   Derivatives Market — 73
The Rise of FX Prime Brokerage — 77
Use of FX Prime Brokerage to Implement Currency Overlay — 79
Prime Brokers Servicing Traditional Asset Managers — 81
The Emergence of 130/30 Strategies — 82
The Advent of the Multi-Prime Brokerage Environment — 84
Factors Responsible for the Trend towards using Multiple
   Prime Brokers — 85
Continued Evolution of Securities Lending Market — 87
Growth of CFD market — 89

7. Cross-Asset Prime Brokerage — 93

Introduction — 94
Foreign Exchange — 94
FX trade process flow — 95
FX Prime Brokerage Deal Process — 98
Evolution of Prime-brokered Trade Execution — 99
Value Proposition — 100
Legal Frameworks and Agreements — 101
Credit Risk Mitigation — 103
Fixed Income — 103

8. Securities Lending — 109

Introduction — 110
Definition of Securities Lending — 110
History of Securities Lending from 1990s — 110
Reasons for Borrowing Securities — 112
The Transaction Life Cycle — 113
Different Types of Securities Lending Transactions — 117
Revenue generation from securities lending — 124
Risks — 125
Settlement Fails — 129
Risk Controls — 129

9. Common Systems Used in Prime Brokerage — 131

Introduction — 132
The Prime Brokerage Technology Market — 133
Profile of systems — 134
List of other systems — 138

10. IT Projects — 141

Introduction — 142
Types of IT Projects — 142
Case Study — 145
Green IT — 148
Building Blocks to a Green IT Strategy — 151

11. Commonly Used Terminology — 157

Introduction — 158
List of Terms — 158

12. The Future — 167

The Future: What does it hold for IT and Business in Prime
Brokerage? — 168
Globalisation of Hedge Funds — 168
Increasing Client Demand — 170
Commoditisation of Prime Brokerage — 171
Consolidation of the Hedge Fund Sector — 171
Evolution of Hedge Fund Business Model — 172
Increasing Use of Technology as a Differentiator — 173
Conclusion — 175

Appendix — 177

List of Useful Websites — 178
Prime Broker Directory — 179
Useful Job Boards — 181
Bibliography — 182

Introduction

The role of technology in enhancing operational efficiencies in the prime brokerage sector, in light of the new expectations of clients, increased regulations and increased competition, cannot be overstated.

This book brings together concepts of business and technology in the prime brokerage world in a way that allows the reader to adopt the mindset of a business-aligned IT professional, capable of supporting business processes and workflows in prime brokerage.

The first chapter provides an overview of prime brokerage – the various definitions and the history as well as a discussion of the global market for prime brokerage services – while Chapter 2 gives a brief overview of hedge funds, the primary clients of prime brokers. Chapter 3 describes the relationship between prime brokers and hedge funds, including the legal underpinnings of the relationship.

Chapters 4 and 5 are essentially about the trading and economic factors affecting the relationship between prime brokers and hedge funds, and the business environment in which prime brokers operate, respectively.

Chapter 6 is about the recent trends shaping the prime brokerage industry while Chapter 7 discusses cross-asset prime brokerage, with emphasis on foreign exchange and fixed income asset classes.

Securities lending is the subject area discussed in depth in Chapter 8. The discussion includes the definition of securities lending, the history of securities, and the motivation for borrowing securities and more. There are also illustrations of different types of securities lending transactions in this chapter.

Chapters 9 and 10 are the more technology-oriented chapters. The common systems used in prime brokerage are showcased in Chapter 9 and also included is a discussion on the prime brokerage technology market. In Chapter 10, the types of IT projects and the developments in technology that are the basis for the execution of IT projects are discussed.

A list of common terminology used in the prime brokerage industry is presented in Chapter 11. In Chapter 12, the final chapter, the future of IT and business in prime brokerage is discussed.

It is advisable to read this book in conjunction with Business Knowledge for IT in Hedge Funds and Business Knowledge for IT in Investment Banking, given that most prime brokers are divisions of investment banks and their main clients are hedge funds. It may also be beneficial for readers to read this book with Business Knowledge for IT in Investment Management, as prime brokers are increasingly seeking to service traditional fund (investment) managers.

Overview of Prime Brokerage

This chapter introduces the concept of prime brokerage and includes the history of prime brokerage and an overview of the global prime brokerage market.

Introduction

Prime brokerage is the name given to a business founded on offering bundled packages of products and services to hedge funds. Prime brokerage products and services are provided by investment banks and large brokerage firms. In broader terms, the prime brokerage business acts as a conduit between hedge funds and the marketplace.

The business benefits to a hedge fund of using a prime broker are that the prime broker offers a centralised securities clearing facility for the hedge fund, and the hedge fund's collateral requirements are netted[1] across all deals handled by the prime broker. The prime broker generates revenue by charging fees on the hedge fund's long and short cash and security positions. Other sources of revenue are the fees charged for clearing and/or other services.

Prime brokers traditionally provided four core services:

1. Clearing, settlement and custody
2. Margin financing
3. Securities lending
4. Consolidated reporting

Nowadays, however, new products and services are being added to the package, such as fund administration, risk analytics, credit intermediation, and initial price offerings (IPO). In addition, a prime broker can allow a client to trade in its name, house and administer client accounts and offer a range of other services such as commission accrual and payment, statement and confirmation generation.

A recent development among prime brokers is the provision of more sophisticated services with a view to becoming a "one-stop shop" for hedge funds. These include start-up services, capital introduction services, front- and back-office systems and technology and cash management services.

Definition of Prime Brokerage

The following are definitions of prime brokerage that capture the essence of the business from different perspectives:

- A provider of a clearing account with credit enhancement. In prime brokerage a client such as a hedge fund reports trades to the prime broker who guarantees and effects settlement of the trade.
- Specialised brokerage services provided by brokers to specific clients who need non-standard services, for example clients who often place orders for very large trades. (Investorwords.com)

---

1 Netting is the settlement of obligations between two parties by processing the combined value of the transactions. It is designed to lower the number of transactions required.

- Prime brokerage is a gateway to a suite of products and services offered by an investment bank to hedge funds, allowing them to operate.

It is important to distinguish between a prime broker that refers to a division of investment banks that offer a package of services to hedge funds, and a broker that refers to any party, bank or otherwise, that mediates between the buyer and seller of any type of security.

History of Prime Brokerage

The stellar growth of hedge funds and their demand for prime brokerage services have boosted the revenues of investment banks in recent times. The anonymous division of investment banks that nobody in the City of London or Wall Street noticed has become one of the most important divisions of the top-tier investment banks. This has not always been so.

The concept and term "prime brokerage" is generally attributed to the US broker-dealer Furman Selz in the late 1970s. Prior to the advent of prime brokerage, portfolio management was a significant challenge; hedge fund managers had to keep track of all of their own trades, consolidate their positions and calculate their performance regardless of which brokerage firms executed those trades or maintained those positions. The concept was immediately seen to be successful, and was quickly copied by the dominant bulge-bracket investment banks.

Prime brokerage emerged in the late 1980s when hedge funds were doggedly focused on returns. At the time, institutionalisation of the business and the focus on asset gathering were not prevalent. Meanwhile, investment banks were trying out new derivative products and other complex securities. There appeared to be a natural fit: hedge funds had the appetite for these new products and investment banks were ready to support them. Ever since then, hedge funds have been among the most well-regarded clients of investment banks, the prime brokerage division being the first point of contact.

Through the 1980s and 1990s, prime brokerage was largely focused on equities, although various prime brokers did supplement their core equities capabilities with basic bond clearing and custody. Additionally, prime brokers provided portfolio reporting to supplement their operational functions; initially by messenger, then by fax and currently over the Internet. Over the years, prime brokers have expanded their product and service offerings to include some or all of the full range of fixed income and derivative products, as well as foreign exchange and futures products.

The explosion of hedge fund services in recent years, especially in Europe, has prompted many US-based prime brokers to establish or boost international prime brokerage platforms. Morgan Stanley was the first to set up an international prime brokerage platform in London in 1989. Goldman Sachs set up its international prime brokerage platform in 1996 while Deutsche Bank started its prime brokerage business in 1999. Another notable entrant into the global prime brokerage space in the 1990s was Barclays Capital, when in 1998 it acquired the equity prime brokerage business of Daiwa.

Given the proliferation of hedge funds across the world in the 1990s and in the current decade, prime brokerage has become fiercely competitive and an important contributor to the overall profitability of the investment banking business. It has become a cornerstone business for the financial markets, on a par with mergers and acquisitions, equity capital markets, and debt and credit markets.

Risk Management for Hedge Funds

Prime brokers offer risk management as a product/service offering to hedge funds. In their role as collateralised lenders, prime brokers have robust monitoring systems in place to protect themselves. In addition, they develop an understanding of their client base, giving them the capabilities to provide a consistent leverage[2] policy to their clients, especially in situations of market disruption and volatility. In some circles, it is perceived as a value-added service, providing a subjective angle on the risks inherent in a portfolio that a manager may wish to consider in comparison to an internal viewpoint. Prime brokers also supply risk aggregation reports as part of their product offerings in response to increased demand from the investor community for risk information flow.

Prime Brokerage Fee Structure

The business of prime brokerage is highly profitable. Fees paid to the banks are huge when compared with standard ones in the fund management industry. In some instances, fees and commission paid by hedge funds for borrowing stock, gearing and trading could be as high as 5% of assets a year, while a typical long-only fund would pay under 0.25% per annum.

The prime brokerage fee structure is derived from three main sources:[3]

1. interest rate spreads on loans to buy shares, bonds or other financial instruments;
2. fees for stock loans to allow hedge funds to sell short; and
3. charges for settling transactions executed elsewhere.

Other services from core businesses such as custody through to dog-walking, advising on schools for managers' children, capital raising and finding office space are usually free of charge.

Evidence of the impact of the fee structure on the bottom line for investment banks is seen in the percentage contributed by prime brokerage to the

---

2 Leverage is the sum of the long and short market values over the equity.
3 Source: Mackintosh, J. (5 March 2007) "How a fledgling has spread its wings", *Financial Times*, FTFM Prime Brokerage.

total revenues of Goldman Sachs (7%) and Morgan Stanley (5%) between 1998 and 2006. Credit Suisse suggested that hedge funds paid $61 billion to the global investment banks equal to 21% of revenue in 2006.[4]

Global Prime Brokerage Market

As the number of hedge funds grew dramatically, from 50 in the 1980s to more than 9,000 at the end of 2007, the growth spurred demand for prime brokerage services at all points of the hedge fund life cycle. Of late, prime brokers have become indispensable partners in a hedge fund strategy for success with their array of service offerings.

The prime brokerage divisions of the major investment banks are now recognised consistent earners for their parent banks. Their success can be attributed to the secrecy surrounding the business, knowledge of profit margins, and the provision of a gamut of products and services to the echelons of the hedge fund marketplace.

Industry experts assert that prime brokerage is about the only segment of the financial markets where banks can still achieve relatively rich spreads because the industry's secrecy hinders the ability of hedge funds to shop around for services and prices.

According to the 2007 Lipper Hedge World Prime Brokerage League Table, Morgan Stanley, Bear Stearns and Goldman Sachs are the prime brokers with the most prime brokerage assets (see Figure 1.1).

However, as of March 2008, Bear Stearns' prime brokerage assets were expected to reduce significantly given the failure of the bank and the subsequent rumoured takeover by JPMorgan Chase. Industry sources claimed that a number of hedge funds moved their money out of Bear Stearns. Prior to this, Goldman Sachs, Morgan Stanley and Bear Stearns together represented 55 to 65% of the market. The market share between these three firms is largely due to their historical commitment to clearing and trading technology.

According to Celent, a US-based consulting firm, global hedge fund assets will grow to US$2.1 trillion by 2009, after an average annual rate of 16.5% from 2005. They expect the growth to sustain demand for prime brokerage services at all stages of the hedge fund life cycle.

Global prime brokerage revenues are expected to reach $11.5 billion by 2009, 230% of the revenues for five years ending 2004, when the value was $5 billion (see Figure 1.3). Figure 1.4 shows the share of the global prime brokerage revenues among the top 10 prime brokerage firms and the others.

If a prime broker can offer complex services across asset classes then it can generate substantial revenues. In equities prime brokerage, for instance, the ability to offer a wide range of complex services can quickly increase revenues. Top prime brokerage platforms can earn 25 to 50 basis points on margin loans

4   Source: Bernstein Research.

Figure 1.1 Prime brokerage assets of leading prime brokers
(in $ billions)

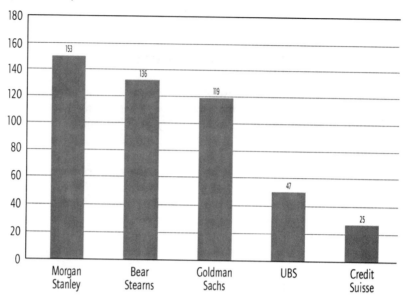

Note: Assets as of year-end 2006.
Source: 2007 Lipper Hedge World Prime Brokerage League Table

Figure 1.2 Market Share of the Global Prime Brokerage Market

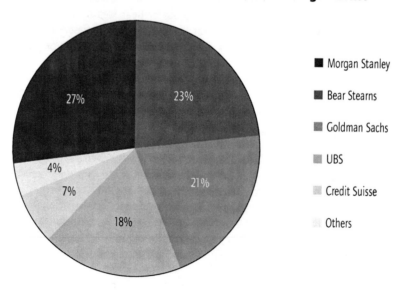

Source: 2007 Lipper Hedge World Prime Brokerage League Table

Figure 1.3 Global prime brokerage revenues (in $ billions)

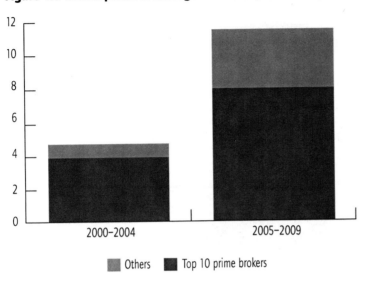

Source: Celent

and 50 to 100 basis points in the case of lending stocks with a large number of shares available. For lending less liquid stocks, the earnings can be 250 basis points according to analysis from Sanford C. Bernstein, a sell-side research firm.

Prime brokers can earn similar revenue from fixed income, by applying a similar pricing matrix.

Revenue generated from securities lending – a service that generates billions for established prime brokers – is expected to diminish in the near future. This is because of the lower margins that newer prime brokers and independent service providers are willing to accept in order to get a piece of the "pie".

The competitive landscape in the securities lending element of the prime brokerage industry derives from two sources: First from professionals in the securities lending and financing industry who have taken a new direction and are setting up their own units. As an example, eSecLending (which auctions securities portfolios to award lending rights to bidders) is a division of Old Mutual, and it is populated with a lot of people that came out of State Street's global lending program.[5] Second are the groups that are known as portfolio financing firms, which act as intermediaries between the hedge fund and a prime broker. These firms are able to acquire their own book to lend directly as well.

Portfolio financing firms act as agents on securities lending transactions in two ways: one as agent and the other as principal. An agent approaches some

---

5   Source: MarHedge, (5 December 2005), Cutthroat Competition, Prime Brokerage Special Report.

Figure 1.4 Share of the Global Prime Brokerage Revenues (2005–2008)

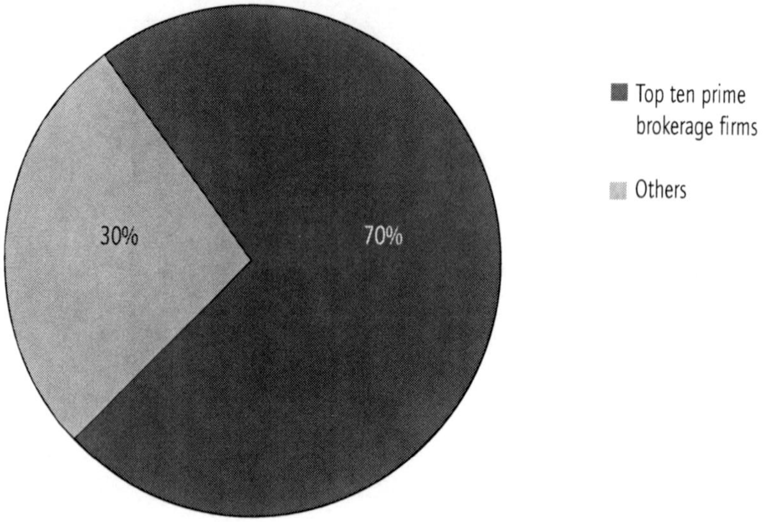

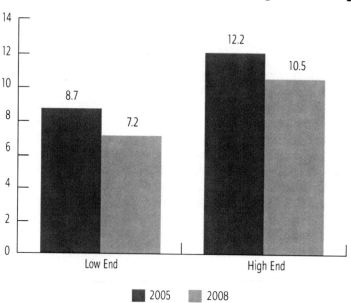

- Top ten prime brokerage firms: 70%
- Others: 30%

Source: Celent

Figure 1.5 Revenue Impact on Securities Lending and Financing (US$B)

	Low End	High End
2005	8.7	12.2
2008	7.2	10.5

Source: Aite Group

firms if they have securities to lend and others about their borrowing needs, and then the two sides are matched up. The second way is for a portfolio financing firm to act as a credit-worthy intermediary – a mini-bank in and of itself that lenders feel comfortable doing business with. That, however, requires having a relatively big balance sheet.

There are other changes afoot in the prime brokerage industry. All players, big and small, will be looking to modernise, innovate and offer cross-asset class services in the face of the emergence of new technologies, growth in derivatives with its associated increase in complexity, and investment bank consolidations.

In addition, given that hedge funds have broadened their investment strategies, established technology platforms are no longer a source of competitive advantage. As stated earlier, hedge fund managers require access to services such as trading, lending, capital introduction, financing and advisory services, but it appears that they now want these services seamlessly and across the globe.

A snag in the predicted growth of the prime brokerage industry is the ease with which fund administrators, technology providers, and even outsourcing firms can duplicate current future service offerings. Despite the close relationship enjoyed by prime brokers with hedge funds from operational and investment perspectives, it is unlikely that hedge funds will give one organisation access to all their investment activity. Furthermore, as hedge funds expand in size, they will probably prefer to either consolidate their operational and administrative activities with a third party or even have them performed internally.

Whilst these revenue figures seem impressive, it is doubtful that they can be sustained in the long term. This is because of the inevitable slowdown of the hedge fund boom as a result of the failure of the less successful funds, and the contraction of prime broker profit margins in the face of increasing expenses.

List of some Prime Brokers

The following are notable investment banks that are known to be providing prime brokerage services:

- Banco Espirito Santo
- Bank of America
- Barclays Capital
- Bear Stearns
- BNP Paribas
- Calyon Financial
- Citigroup
- CIBC World Markets
- Credit Suisse
- Deutsche Bank
- Dresdner Kleinwort
- Fidelity Investments

- Fortis
- Goldman Sachs
- Interactive Brokers
- Jefferies & Company
- JPMorgan Chase
- Lehman Brothers
- Merrill Lynch
- Morgan Stanley
- Newedge Group (ex Fimat & Calyon Financial)
- RBS
- RBC Capital Markets
- Rabobank
- Triad Securities
- UBS

Overview of Hedge Funds

This chapter introduces the concept of hedge funds, the global market and the source of investments. Also included is a range of strategies that hedge fund managers typically pursue.

Introduction

Hedge funds are the major benefactors of prime brokers. The recent reversal of the fortunes of the prime brokerage industry is mainly due to the explosive growth of the hedge fund industry in recent years. Prime brokerage as a service function was not until recently a widely known sector of the financial services industry. The only people who were aware of their services were those that had affiliations with the hedge fund industry.

In Chapter 3 there will be a detailed discussion on the relationship between hedge funds and prime brokers, but it is useful to provide an overview of hedge funds in this chapter as a background.

What are Hedge Funds?

Hedge funds are investment vehicles that take big bets on a wide range of assets and specialise in sophisticated investment techniques. Some of these funds have made huge amounts of money for their investors in recent years. They are meant to perform well in falling as well as rising markets.

Hedge funds are defined by their structure rather than any specific investment method. They are set up as limited partnerships in which the manager acts as the general partner while the investor acts as the limited partner. Strangely, the term "hedge fund" is a misnomer as not all hedge funds are hedged. Hedge funds invest in any number of strategies regardless of the common term that attempts to enclose them. These strategies include investing in asset classes such as stocks, commodities, and currency mechanisms that boost return such as derivatives, leverage and arbitrage.

Hedge funds are involved in a wide range of activities that are only limited by prevailing contractual obligations of the particular fund. As a consequence, they use a wide range of complex and specialist investment strategies. The most commonly used is going long or short on a share.

A conventional method that private investors adopt is to go long on a share, in the hope that by buying the share they will make a profit when the price rises. However, in the situation where an investor goes short, they expect the equity will fall in value. Hedge funds take two principal approaches to achieve this. In the first instance the fund manager "shorts" the stock, where the investor "borrows" a stock to sell it, hoping that it will decrease in value so that they can buy it back at a lower price and profit from the difference.

To illustrate this, if an investor borrows 2,000 shares of a company called Biz Telecoms at £20 each, they would sell those for £40,000. If the price falls to, say, £18 per share, the investor would buy the shares back for £36,000, return them to the original owner, and make a profit of £4,000.

Another approach for exploiting falling share prices is to deal in "contracts for difference" (CFD).[6] This provides an opportunity for the investor to make money on share price movements without actually buying the shares.

Hedge funds have a reputation for secrecy given that in most countries they are prohibited from marketing to non-accredited investors, unlike regulated retail investment funds such as mutual funds and pension funds. As hedge funds are essentially a private pool of managed assets, and as their public access is commonly restricted by governments in most countries, they have little or no incentive to release their private information to the public.

A lot of hedge funds are run by former investment bankers and traditional fund managers who set up their own funds. As a result of their risky profiles and the lack of regulations for hedge funds, they only accept investments from wealthy, sophisticated investors and hence charge them very high fees. The fees are typically a 2% management fee as well as 20% of the profits, making the hedge fund managers a lot of money.

Hedge funds are classed as alternative investments, which are increasingly being viewed as comparatively safe methods of diversification.

Definition of Hedge Funds

Many descriptions have been used to define a hedge fund, despite the difficulty of defining a generic term that is used loosely to cover a variety of trading strategies. Nevertheless, the following are some explicit definitions of hedge funds:

- A hedge fund is a fund that can take both long and short positions, use arbitrage, buy and sell undervalued securities, trade options or bonds, and invest in almost any opportunity in any market where it foresees impressive gains at reduced risk.
- Hedge funds are private pooled investment limited partnerships which fall outside many of the rules and regulations of mutual funds. Hedge funds therefore can invest in a variety of securities on a leveraged basis. In recent times, the term hedge fund refers not so much to the hedging techniques that hedge funds may employ as it does to their status as private investment partnerships. (IFSL)
- A hedge fund is an aggressively managed portfolio of investments that uses advanced investment strategies such as leverage, long, short and derivative positions in both domestic and international markets with the goal of generating high returns (either in an absolute sense or over a specified market benchmark). (Investopedia)

---

6   A CFD on a company's shares specifies the price of the shares when the contract was started. The contract is an agreement to pay out the cash on the difference between the starting share price and the price when the contract is closed.

- A hedge fund is a term commonly used to describe any fund that isn't a conventional investment fund – that is, any fund using a strategy or set of strategies other than investing long in bonds, equities (mutual funds), and money markets (money market funds).

Key Characteristics of Hedge Funds

- Hedge funds utilise a variety of financial instruments to reduce risk, enhance returns and minimise the correlation with equity and bond markets. Many hedge funds are flexible in their investment options (can use short selling, leverage, derivatives such as puts, calls, options, futures, etc.).
- Hedge funds vary enormously in terms of investment returns, volatility and risk. Many, but not all, hedge fund strategies tend to hedge against downturns in the markets being traded.
- Many hedge funds have the ability to deliver non-market-correlated returns.
- Many hedge funds have consistency of returns and capital preservation as objectives rather than magnitude of returns.
- Most hedge funds are managed by experienced investment professionals who are generally disciplined and diligent.
- Hedge funds represent a distinctive investment style and objectives. Their strategies differ greatly from traditional funds.
- Hedge fund management companies are usually small organisations controlled by one or two key investment professionals.
- The money manager–client relationship in hedge funds is a radical departure from the traditional relationship in that the client does not merely hire the manager, instead the client has input into the investment process like a partner, co-investing in the situations that the manager finds attractive.
- Hedge funds utilise unique "structures" to deliver their strategies to their investors. These structures could take the form of a limited partnership, a commodity pool, an offshore fund, or a specialised kind of separate account.
- Pension funds, endowments, insurance companies, private banks and high net worth individuals and families invest in hedge funds to minimise overall portfolio volatility and enhance returns.
- Most hedge fund managers are highly specialised and trade only within their area of expertise and competitive advantage.
- Hedge funds benefit by heavily weighting hedge fund managers' remuneration towards performance incentives, thus attracting the best brains in the investment business. In addition, hedge fund managers usually have their own money invested in their fund.
- Hedge funds are exempt from many investment protection and disclosure requirements as the majority of hedge funds are domiciled offshore or subject to limited regulations by onshore regulators.

Reasons for Investing in Hedge Funds

There are different reasons for investors deciding to invest in hedge funds. Some of them are:

- **To increase the return on the portfolio** – The fact that hedge funds have done well irrespective of the aggregate for a given industry is a compelling reason for investors to turn to them. Hedge fund performance is comparatively better than traditional investments.
- **To diversify the returns of assets within a portfolio** – Another major reason investors are drawn to hedge funds is diversification which involves correlation, a statistical measure of how two securities move in relation to each other. Investors clearly appreciate the benefits of diversification as they are aware that stocks don't always move together and a portfolio can be less risky than its constituent stocks.
- **To reduce risk** – Individual and institutional investors also invest in hedge funds to reduce the risk of their overall portfolio. Despite the role that diversification plays in risk reduction, without the obvious benefits, a lot of hedge funds have lower risk than traditional assets. One of the characteristics of hedge funds that investors are aware of is a measure of risk called volatility.[7] Even without the benefits of diversification, hedge funds can lower the return volatility of a portfolio without lowering its expected return.

Types of Hedge Fund Strategies

Hedge funds use a range of strategies that offer different levels of risk and return but their main aim is to preserve capital and to generate positive returns in all conditions, including falling markets. Hedge funds invest in almost every class including equities, fixed income, currencies and commodities, depending on their strategies.

Hedge fund managers typically have greater flexibility in their investment options than traditional investment managers who follow more conventional strategies. Hedge funds adopt aggressive strategies and are able to borrow funds. Given their need to react to short-term market movements to achieve their objectives, hedge funds trade frequently.

There are many different ways to classify the investment strategies of hedge fund managers. However, some managers combine a number of strategies in what are known as "multi-strategy funds". Hedge fund style allocation, according to the following strategies, is shown in Figure 2.1.

The following are illustrations of the four main categories: relative value,

---

7   A statistical measure of the dispersion of returns for a given security or market index. Volatility can be measured by using either the standard deviation or variance between returns from that same security or market index.

Figure 2.1 Hedge Fund Industry Style Allocation

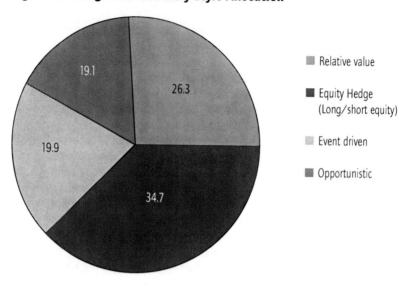

Source: Hedge Fund Research, Inc. (HFRI). As at 30 September 2006.

event-driven, long/short equity and opportunistic, and the sub-categories of investment strategies.

1 Relative Value
- **Fixed income arbitrage** – This is a strategy that involves a hedge fund manager profiting from the exploitation of the pricing inefficiencies between related fixed income securities while seeking to neutralise exposure to interest rate risk. This strategy is often leveraged in the quest for higher returns.
- **Convertible arbitrage** – Ordinarily, this strategy involves buying a convertible bond and at the same time hedging a portion of the equity risk by selling short the underlying common stock. The strategy typically benefits from three different sources:
  - interest earned on the cash earned from the short sales of equities;
  - coupon offered by the bond convertible; and
  - so-called "gamma".

  The gamma element is the result of the change in volatility of the underlying equity and involves frequent trading. This strategy is also usually leveraged in the quest for higher returns.
- **Statistical arbitrage** – This strategy seeks to profit from pricing inefficiencies between securities. This is usually identified through mathematical modelling methods. The rationale behind pursuing a statistical arbitrage strategy is the notion that prices will return to their historical norms. This

strategy is also typically leveraged in the quest for higher returns.

2 Event-driven

▨ **Risk arbitrage** – This is also commonly referred to as merger arbitrage as the strategy invests in merger situations. This strategy involves the simultaneous purchase and sale of the stocks of two merging companies to create a riskless profit. The strategy can also be expressed as one that consists of being long on the stock of the target company while simultaneously selling short the stock of the acquiring the company.

▨ **Special situations** – This strategy seeks to profit from opportunities created as a result of corporate life-cycle events such as spin-offs, mergers, acquisitions, green mail[8] transactions and management changes.

▨ **Distressed securities** – This strategy involves investing in companies that are reorganising. This reorganisation involves the restructuring of the debt portion of their balance sheet. This type of strategy also consists of buying securities of companies in bankruptcy proceedings. The complex nature of such activities often creates opportunities for hedge fund managers to exploit mispricing of the securities of these types of companies to gain high returns.

3 Long/ short Equity

▨ **Growth/ value/ industry/ geographical/ capitalisation** – This is an opportunistic directional strategy that combines both long and short positions on stocks. The strategy entails the opportunistic adjustment of the net market exposure. The hedge fund manager can diversify holdings across market capitalisations, industries and countries.

▨ **Short sellers** – Hedge fund managers use short-selling strategies to attempt to profit from falls in the value of stocks. The method for achieving the profits entails buying a stock and selling it on the market with the aim of buying it back at a lower price at a later date. The cash proceeds from the short sale is invested and the hedge fund manager receives interest.

▨ **Market neutral** – This is a strategy that is pursued with a view to exploiting inefficiencies in the equity markets by profiting from both increasing and decreasing prices in a single or numerous markets. Market-neutral strategies are often achieved by taking matching long and short positions in different stocks to increase the return from making good stock selections and decrease the loss from broad market movements. A market-neutral position may involve taking a 50% long, 50% short position in a particular industry, such as pharmaceuticals, or taking the same position in the broader market.

---

8   It occurs when publicly traded companies are forced to buy back shares, at a premium to the current trading price, from large investors or corporate raiders in order to maintain their independence.

4 Opportunistic

- ▪ **Macro** – This is a strategy whereby fund managers take out positions on the fixed income, equity, currency and commodity markets via either direct investments or futures and other types of derivative products on the basis of in-depth analyses of macro-economic trends.
- ▪ **Managed funds** – This strategy entails investment in futures contracts on financial commodity and currency markets on a global basis. Managers base trading decisions on proprietary quantitative models and technical analysis. This strategy is also known as CTA which stands for Commodity Trading Advisors.

Fee Structure

The fee structure of hedge funds is such that fees are significantly higher and considerably more complicated that those of registered investment companies.

The following are types of fees charged by hedge funds.

Management Fee

Hedge funds, in common with other investment funds, charge a management fee. This fee is assessed based on the assets under management. The fee is usually at an annual rate between 1% and 2% of the net asset value (NAV) of the fund. However, since investors are allowed to enter and exit the funds at any time of the year, the fees are generally assessed monthly and in some cases more frequently.

Performance Fee

Performance fees provide an avenue for hedge fund managers to share in the positive returns of a fund. This is one of the major characteristics of hedge funds. Performance fees are typically 20% of gross returns and exist as an incentive for the fund manager to perform well.

The rationale behind performance fees is to align the interest of manager and investor better than flat fees that are paid to the manager even if performance is poor.

Surrender Fee

Hedge funds charge a surrender fee, which is a percentage of the redemption amount for investors who wish to leave the fund. In some cases, this fee is paid back into the fund as compensation to the remaining investors for the transaction costs associated with the liquidation of assets for the redemption. This fee, when paid to the management company, acts as a deterrent to other investors who may be considering leaving the fund and also generates additional revenue for the fund.

Hurdle Fee

Some funds specify a hurdle rate, which is a variant of the performance fee, whereby the fund will not charge a performance fee until its annualised performance exceeds a benchmark rate, such as Treasury bills or fixed percentage, over some period. This links performance fees to the ability of the manager to do better than the investor would have done if they had put their money in a bank account.

It should be noted that this practice has diminished as demand for hedge funds has outstripped supply and hurdle rates are now rare.

World's 10 Best Hedge Funds

Table 2.1 List of the world's 10 best hedge funds as of April 2008

Fund Name	Strategy	3-Year Annual Return (%)	2007 Return (%)	Company Name	Total Firm Assets ($billions)
Passport II-Global	Equity Long/ Short	65.50	219.44	Passport Capital	3.7
Dynamic Power	Event Driven	60.20	38.60	Goodman and Company	26.6
Paulson Enhanced	Merger Arbitrage	50.66	129.13	Paulson & Co.	29.0
Balestra Capital Partners	Diversified Long/Short	48.59	199.14	Balestra Capital	0.7
Renaissance Technologies Medallion Fund	Quantitative Trading	48.10	73.70	Renaissance Technologies	30.0
Metage Special Emerging Market	Emerging Market Equity	46.81	61.65	Metage Capital	N/A
Atticus European – Class A	Multi-Strategy	44.38	27.86	Atticus Management	N/A
Harbinger Capital Partners Flagship Fund	Global Distressed Securities	43.90	116.10	Harbinger Capital Partners	18.0
Children's Investment Fund	Equity/Long Short	41.98	37.59	Children's Investment Fund Management	5.0
Aisling Analytics Merchant Commodity Fund	Discretionary	39.99	36.91	Aisling Analytics	N/A

Source: Barron's

Figure 2.2 Global Hedge Funds

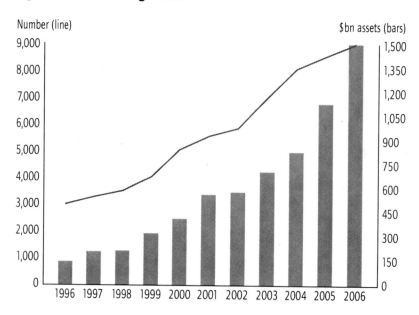

Source: IFSL estimates based on various sources

High-water Mark

Although performance fees are normally not refunded following a loss, the investors are usually protected so that the hedge fund manager earns no fee for making back a loss. In a typical structure, returns are determined by the net asset value (NAV) of a unit of participation in a fund. Each time the NAV reaches a new high level, the performance fee is calculated. When the NAV reduces in the event of a loss, no performance fee is calculated until the NAV exceeds the highest NAV used for performance fee assessment. Some funds maintain high-water marks for each individual investor and may trace multiple high-water marks on individuals if they add to their investments after a loss.

Lookback Fee

Although not a classic fee structure, some management companies refund a performance fee if an ensuing loss wipes out a gain not long after the performance fee payment, when losses are incurred within three months of the high-water mark.

Miscellaneous Fee

The management company may charge a variety of fees at their discretion, if they are adequately disclosed to the investors. The fund can be charged a ticket charge for purchases and sales handled by the management company. A financing fee is sometimes charged for handling leveraged long and short financing transactions for leverage positions.

Global Hedge Fund Industry

Hedge funds have grown rapidly in recent years and while the market is showing signs of maturing, institutional portfolio allocations into hedge funds have helped the rise in the number and assets of these funds. The key driver behind this growth was the ability of hedge funds – once the preserve of high net worth individuals – to deliver absolute returns in falling markets. This was a major draw to institutional investors.

There is a wider availability of "fund of hedge funds" products as a result of changes to national regulations and the EU-wide Undertakings for Collective Investment in Transferable Securities (UCITS III).

It is difficult to determine the exact size of the hedge fund industry as estimates vary due to the restrictions imposed on advertising and reporting of performance by hedge funds. However, according to International Financial Services, London: "Assets under management of the global hedge fund industry totalled around $1,500bn at the end of 2006." This figure represents a 33% increase on corresponding figures for 2005 and nearly 50% increase over 2003's figures. Hedge funds usually use leverage and so take positions in financial markets that are larger than their assets under management.

In terms of net assets, a record $126bn of new money flowed into the global hedge fund industry in 2006, which is about a 200% increase on the amount of money raised in 2005. This follows a gradual decline in inflow between 2002 and 2005. In Europe, new hedge fund launches raised a record $38bn in 2006, up a third on 2005.

The following is further interesting information about the global hedge fund industry:

- Hedge funds can be registered in onshore and offshore locations; the most popular locations being the Cayman Islands followed by the British Virgin Islands and Bermuda.
- In 2006, the USA was the most popular onshore location (with funds mostly registered in Delaware), which accounted for 48% of the number of onshore funds, followed by Ireland with 7%.
- New York is the world's leading location for hedge fund managers and is home to half of the domiciled hedge fund managers. It is estimated that 36% of global hedge funds assets were managed in New York in 2006.
- London is the second largest global centre for hedge fund managers with a 21% share of the global hedge fund industry.
- At the end of 2006, around 80% of European hedge fund investments totalling $460bn were managed out of the UK, the vast majority from London.
- There were around 1,400 European-based hedge funds in 2006, of which 66% were located in London. Other locations for hedge funds in Europe include Spain, France and Switzerland.

- Asia, especially China, is gaining importance in the global hedge fund industry. Australia was the main centre for the management of Asia-Pacific hedge funds in 2006.
- Australia-based hedge fund managers accounted for around 25% of the $140bn in Asia-Pacific hedge fund assets in 2006.
- Other important locations for Asian hedge fund management include Japan and Hong Kong.

Source of Investments

In recent years there has been a marked increase in investment from institutional investors into hedge funds. These include pension funds, universities, endowments and charitable organisations. This is in contrast to the 1990s when most hedge fund investments came from high net worth individuals.

Institutional investors accounted for 37% of the stock of single hedge fund manager investments at the end of 2006, a 12% increase when compared to 1997. Also, in 2005 around 2% of global institutional portfolio assets were invested in hedge funds. Although high net worth individuals increased their

Figure 2.3 Global Hedge Funds by Source of Funds

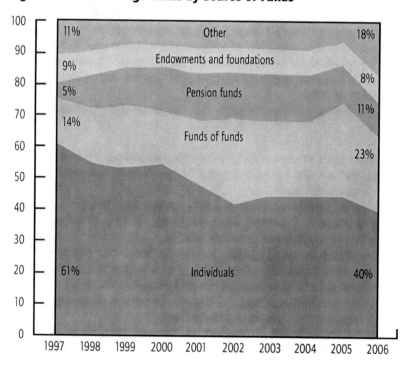

Source: Hennessee Group LLC

allocation to hedge funds between 1996 and 2006, their share of the total declined from 61% in 1997 to 40% in 2006 as a result of the rise in institutional capital.

Institutional investors from the USA accounted for 41% of global institutional hedge fund investment in 2005, with European and Japanese investors accounting for 44%. Most institutional investors invest in hedge funds through funds of hedge funds and more recently through multi-strategy managers. A Greenwich Associates survey shows that in 2006, 13% of UK pension funds invested in hedge funds. As a result, 1.1% of UK pension funds' assets are invested in hedge funds, with 24% of pension funds planning to increase their exposure to hedge funds by 2008. UK institutional investors invest less into their alternative investments than some other European countries.

Figure 2.4 Institutional Hedge Fund Assets by Country/ Region

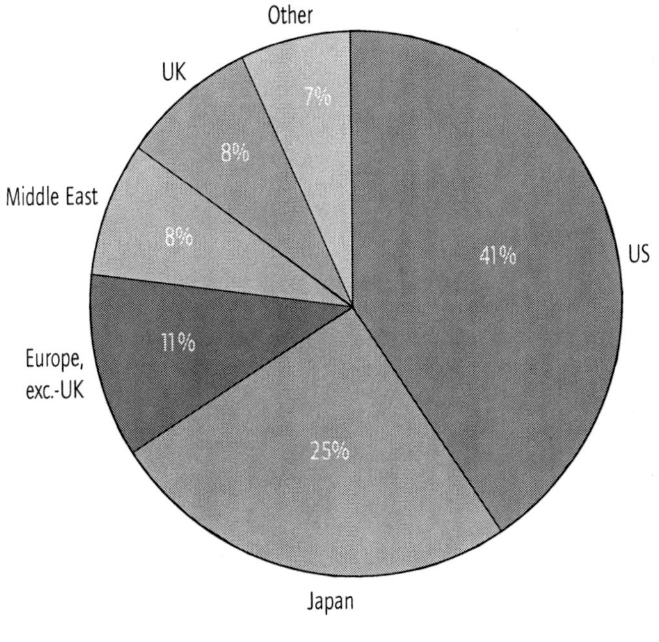

Source: *The Bank of New York and Casey, Quirk & Associates analysis*

The Relationship between Prime Brokers and Hedge Funds

3

This chapter discusses the relationship between prime brokers and their foremost clients – hedge funds.

Introduction

Industry experts opine that not all hedge funds require the services of a prime broker. Only a hedge fund that needs to borrow securities requires their services and a hedge fund that has a trading strategy involving the buying and selling of exchange traded derivative instruments has no need of a prime broker. Such hedge funds deal directly in exchange traded contracts (with no requirement to borrow securities).

Some hedge funds operate without prime brokers choosing, for instance, to execute deals via contracts for difference, bought from broker. However, some experts believe that if a hedge fund disintermediates all the prime broker functions, it will have an effect on the intangible services that the prime broker offers.

Nevertheless, hedge funds establish prime brokerage relationships to minimise operational and accounting-related issues, and to rein in costs through consolidated financing, while maintaining the merits of executing with a number of brokers. When a fund appoints a prime broker, it instructs all its executing brokers to settle its trades for cash with a single firm.

After a fund executes a trade, it forwards the details to its prime broker. The prime broker clear the trade, holds the securities for safekeeping, provides margin financing, lends stock to cover short sales, and provides cash and position reports and technology.

When the prime broker is said to clear transactions of a hedge fund, it means that it confirms the trade with the hedge fund's counterparties on the night of the trade. Should there be any discrepancy between what the customer reports and what is in the prime brokerage system, the prime broker is responsible for communicating this to the customer on the morning of the trade date plus one (T+1) and for settling any differences.

Role of the Prime Broker

In the past, prime brokerage was perceived as a purely operational function, responsible for clearing and settling trades, custody, and reporting of a hedge fund's trades (see Figure 3.1). However, nowadays prime brokers continue to offer these services and have added some additional services such as capital introduction, consulting and risk management amongst others.

Overview of Products and Services offered by Prime Brokers

The proliferation of hedge funds and their more prominent role in the capital markets has led prime brokers to gradually overhaul their product and service offerings in order to satisfy hedge funds' exacting requirements. As stated ear-

Figure 3.1 The Role of a Prime Broker

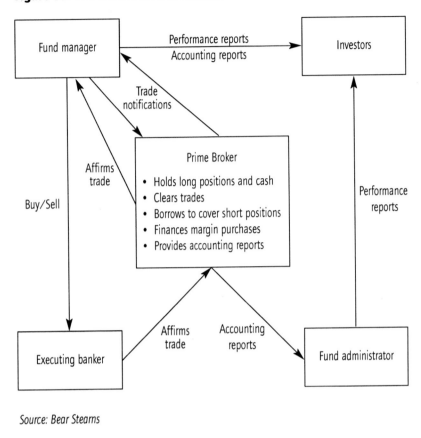

Source: Bear Stearns

lier, prime brokers' core services include consolidated reporting, securities lending, margin financing and clearing, settlement and custody. In the current hedge fund marketplace, this means providing a core service that gives hedge funds access to a vast array of markets and products, such as fixed income securities, currencies, commodities, equities and derivatives such as futures, options and swaps.

A prime broker can be said to be a gateway between hedge funds and the marketplace. The prime broker often assumes the role of clearer on behalf of the fund and financier for the fund's transactions, and provides custody services and also securities lending for short sales. One of the major benefits that hedge funds derive from using a prime broker is that they are able to maintain a master account for consolidating their securities and cash balances when trading with multiple brokers (see Figure 3.2). Ancillary services offered to hedge funds with master accounts include margin financing, consolidated reporting and back-office processing.

Figure 3.2 Hedge Fund *With/Without* Primer Broker

1. Hedge Fund *without* Prime Broker

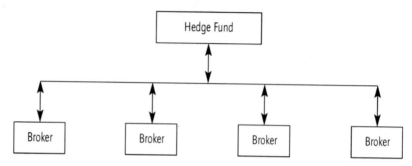

2. Hedge Fund *with* Prime Broker

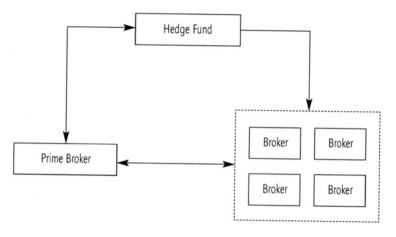

Source: Aima, Canada

Core Services

- **Clearance and settlement** – The process begins when a hedge fund trades with an executing broker/dealer.[9] The entire process, known in the industry as "give-up", involves a hedge fund entering into the trade and the fund supplying the executing broker with the prime broker's name and the details of the relevant account with the prime broker.

---

9   The broker or dealer that completes and processes an order on behalf of a client. Before an executing broker carries out the order, it assesses it for appropriateness and if found to be practical, executes the order.

Details of the trade the hedge fund enters into include the following:

- Instrument name
- Quantity of the security to be traded
- Price
- Time of trade

The executing broker then gives up the trade and the related trade details to the prime broker. As part of the process, the hedge fund also forwards the details of the trade (including any allocation of the trade) to the prime broker. The trade details are then reconciled to uncover any mismatches. If the trade details match, confirmation is the next step and it involves the prime broker confirming the trade with the executing broker. If there are mismatches, however, the prime broker and the executing broker then work together to remedy the situation.

The prime broker can assume the role of principal or agent in the give-up process. In its role as an agent, the prime broker clears and settles, typically, exchange or cash securities on behalf of the hedge fund, doing away with the associated counterparty risk. When acting as a principal, the prime broker is permitting the hedge fund to trade under its name and acts as an intermediary of a sort by assuming the role of the hedge fund when dealing with the executing broker, as well as assuming the role of the executing broker when dealing with the hedge fund with regards to future cash flow associated with the trade. Principal prime brokerage is most associated with credit, foreign exchange and OTC derivative markets.

- **Custody** – The prime broker is entrusted with the safe custody of all the assets (cash, securities, contracts and claims) and it holds these assets in an account set apart from the accounts of the prime broker, its other customers and affiliates.
- **Financing and margining** – Prime brokers provide financing to their hedge fund clients so that they can attain the leverage[10] required for their chosen strategies. The prime broker uses different criteria, which include a combination of value-at-risk and stress-testing to assess the amount of leverage to extend to their hedge fund clients and this is on a portfolio-by-portfolio, or in some cases, client-by-client basis.

The hedge funds use leverage in a variety of ways depending on their investment strategy. For instance, for an opportunistic strategy, the leverage could be about 10% while equity market neutral could require leverage of about 15%.

In the prime brokerage industry, leverage offered to hedge fund clients can be approached in two ways – by the use of derivatives and through margin financing.

---

10 The amount of debt used to finance a hedge fund's assets. The degree of leverage is dependent on the debt to equity ratio.

Financing by means of derivatives is achieved in different ways. One commonly used approach is a managed account swap. This involves the prime broker setting up an account managed and advised by the hedge fund manager who has trading discretion.[11] The prime broker and the hedge fund engage in a total return swap transaction which in effect transfers the economics of the account of the fund. The hedge fund manager receives the returns associated with the account by trading the account in order to implement the hedge fund's strategy. The hedge fund also needs to post an amount of margin on the swap based on the leverage used by the fund.

The following example illustrates this scenario.

BBU, a fictional prime broker, has an account of £200 million of its own assets. This account is advised by BizFund (fictional hedge fund manager) and BizFund is also the counterparty to a total return swap on the account. BBU requires BizFund to post £25 million of equity as margin for the swap.

Leverage used by BizFund is therefore 8 to 1 (i.e. 200/25).

The other method is to extend margin[12] financing. This facility allows the hedge fund to borrow some fraction of a security from the prime broker.

This is illustrated in the following example. Supposing BizFund holds a long position of a portfolio of securities with a value of £60 million financed by £40 million of margin debt and £20 million of equity, then the leverage can be expressed as 3 to 1 (i.e. 60/20).

■ **Securities lending** – Securities lending is the temporary transfer of securities by one party to another on a collateralised basis. It is one of the more important services that prime brokers provide to their hedge fund clients. Prime brokers are the main source of those securities for hedge funds.

The process of securities lending begins with the prime broker approaching a lender, who is usually an investor[13] that is willing to allow its securities to be loaned out. The prime broker then pledges collateral to the lender in order to secure the lending facility. The hedge fund now obtains the security from the prime broker and sells short in the marketplace. The revenue generated from the short sale[14] can be used to finance the acquisition of other securities, provided that the prime broker's margin requirements are met by the portfolio of securities for which the hedge fund is a custodian. More on securities lending in Chapter 8.

■ **Record keeping** – In order to comply with regulations, it is imperative for a prime broker to maintain records and books that are associated with each hedge fund account they manage. The prime broker must ensure that all

---

11 A trading discretion allows the hedge fund manager to amend a limit order according to their own judgement, allowing them to buy or sell to a set point beyond the bounds of the original order. A limit order is an order placed with a brokerage to buy or sell a set number of shares at a specified price or better.

12 Margin is the money that the hedge fund will borrow to purchase securities.

13 The investor could be a pension fund, a custody bank or mutual fund.

14 Short sale is the sale of the borrowed security.

portfolio-related information, including: trades and positions, position profit and loss, interest and dividends and corporate actions are accurately recorded.

- **Reporting and statements** – Prime brokers produce statements and reports for their hedge fund clients as a by-product of record keeping. Amongst the reports produced are daily transaction reports, margin reports, cash balance reports and other information related to the activity of the hedge fund. Depending on the requirements of the client, the reports can be produced in both electronic and paper-based formats.

Ancillary Services

- **Trade execution** – One increasingly popular service that prime brokers offer their hedge fund clients is trade execution, either through their facilities or through the facilities of one of their affiliates. This service is in addition to the hedge fund's ability to execute trades with a variety of counterparties, facilitated by prime brokers.
- **Derivative support** – Prime brokers give their hedge fund clients access to their derivatives desk for trading and risk management ideas.
- **Research** – This is a service that is provided to hedge funds by allowing them access to in-house reports.
- **Enhanced leverage** – Hedge funds have access to lines of credit from prime brokers that they can use for leverage.
- **Fund administration and/or trustee services** – This is an outsourced service that some prime brokers offer to their hedge fund clients.
- **Capital introduction** – This service offering entails introducing hedge fund clients to potential investors and new sources of capital through the private banking and asset management functions of the parent investment bank.
- **IPO or issuance access** – Hedge funds that use multiple prime brokers are aware of the benefits this offers by way of access to the flow of initial public offerings (IPOs) from these brokers. Some hedge fund strategies, such as convertible arbitrage, depend on the issuance of securities; therefore this access engenders their relationship with a prime broker.
- **Start-up services** – Some start-up hedge funds require special services such as office space, introduction to legal, administrator and accounting service providers, and technological support and many prime brokers provide these as part of their service offerings.
- **Consulting services** – There are varying degrees of consulting services that prime brokers offer to their hedge fund clients ranging from human resources, employment practices and recruitment to technology-related services such as hardware and software purchases and installation.
- **Office space** – As stated above, prime brokers offer office space to their hedge fund clients. This is usually on a cost plus basis whereby a prime broker acquires office space and sublets the space to the hedge fund clients. The advantage to the hedge fund is the ability to rent space at reduced costs, given that the prime broker has greater purchasing power and uses it to negotiate for a larger amount of space.

■ **Risk and performance analytics** – Some prime brokers are able to provide their hedge fund clients with access to daily risk analysis, performance analysis and reporting by forming strategic alliances with risk management services such as the RiskMetrics Group.

Risk Management for Hedge Funds

Prime brokers offer risk management as a product/service offering to hedge funds. In their role as collateralised lenders, prime brokers have robust monitoring systems in place to protect themselves. In addition, they develop an understanding of their client base, giving them the capabilities to provide consistent leverage[15] policy to their clients, especially in situations of market disruption and volatility. In some circles, it is perceived as a value-added service, providing a subjective angle on the risks inherent in a portfolio that a manager may wish to consider in comparison to an internal viewpoint. Prime brokers also supply risk aggregation reports as part of their product offering in response to increased demand from the investor community for risk information flow.

In addition, risk is essential for institutional investors establishing a hedge fund strategy. Prime brokers have been conversant with the risk of hedge fund investments and have managed this risk for years. Usually, the prime broker puts up the money for the investments and, hence, they are often the fund's largest financial stakeholder. Without doubt, prime brokers are concerned with risk management and their needs are similar to those of the institutional investor.

As shown earlier, prime brokers provide an array of products and services to hedge funds. This gives them complete transparency on the fund. The provision of these services positions a prime broker in a unique way, enabling it to carry out the necessary risk management policies and procedures.

Managing risk for hedge fund investments is not unlike assessing investment risk in traditional asset managers.

A prime broker uses a comprehensive risk assessment matrix to help measure and monitor the risk involved in a hedge fund. An example of this type of approach is a framework that utilises the "Four Ps", namely people, processes, portfolio and performance. People and processes utilise micro/quantative criteria, while portfolio characteristics and performance utilise micro/quantitative criteria.

Under each category, there is a checklist of criteria that are assessed on a pre-qualification and/or ongoing basis. Weightings are applied to each category and scores are assigned to these criteria to reflect the level of satisfaction. The final total is compared with a benchmark score so as to determine whether a prospective hedge fund meets the risk parameters.

The main aim within the "people" segment of the checklist is to determine whether the hedge fund has strong financial backers and to determine if the

---

15 Leverage is the sum of the long and short market values over the equity.

Figure 3.3 Four Ps Framework

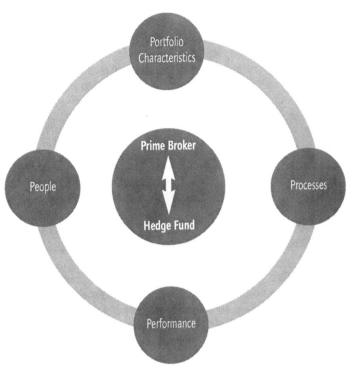

© Essvale Corporation Limited, 2008.

principals of the firm have made substantial personal investment in the fund. This demonstrates their commitment and confidence in the business and can be a useful indicator.

The next aspect to look at is how strong the management team is and if there are synergies that the key players bring to the running of the fund, such as expertise, leadership and skill.

The main concern within the "process" segment is to determine the investment strategy being pursued and to estimate its probability of success based on the strategy's past performance and expected performance in the context of the current and expected market outlook.

Additionally, other elements that can be looked at are the trading model being employed, the adequacy of the documentation (i.e. legal agreements, investment policies and operational procedures) and the sufficiency of management's control and oversight of the investment and operations activities.

The "portfolio characteristics" aspect requires a firm understanding and overview of the fund's daily transactions and positions so as to perform in-depth analytical calculations reflecting its financial strengths. Traditional accounting and market ratios such as leverage, liquidity, margin, value-at-risk (VAR) and correlation are measured and compared to a suitable benchmark in order to determine the risk exposure on a daily basis. Corrective actions (increasing margins, liquidation of certain positions, etc.) may be required to realign the portfolio balance sheet.

Prime brokers often undertake thorough reviews of both past results and projected performance in order to appraise the likelihood that the fund will be able to produce the projected return and to assess the fund with regards to survival risk. The historical monthly returns over the life of the fund, the consistency of returns over some money market benchmarks, and the growth of capital raised are some of the considerations of the review.

Prime brokers have cottoned on to the fact that applying basic approaches to assessing traditional asset managers and identifying the unique characteristics of a hedge fund are essential to clarifying and demystifying hedge fund risk.

What Hedge Funds Want from Prime Brokers

Hedge fund managers are so dependent upon their prime broker that any weakness in its service could have ruinous ramifications. Therefore, a manager should consider all aspects of the services required when selecting the prime broker. However, for a start, they must be fully at ease that the prime broker is not just financially secure but, in today's markets, very solid and very well capitalised. This is very crucial in the current business environment whereby it seems that everyone who has a balance sheet and the ability to clear a trade is offering prime broker services. The question is, what qualities are hedge fund managers looking for when selecting a prime broker?

The following are some of the qualities that hedge funds desire in a prime broker:

- **Understanding of both the hedge fund business and the business of prime brokerage** – Hedge funds want a prime broker that understands their strategy, how they implement these strategies, and all the parameters of their business. They also would want reassurance that the prime broker is able to service their entire business.
- **Autonomy from the trading division** – Hedge funds want a broker whose sole function is prime brokerage. Some prime brokers are sub-units of trading divisions of investment banks and this could change the dynamics of the relationship between them and the hedge funds for the worse. Hedge funds would like a situation whereby the confidentiality of their trading activity or position is maintained.
- **Understanding of the risk of the fund's strategy and the effective management of its exposure** – Hedge funds want a prime broker to have a global risk management organisation that understands their style and trading strategy. This is important for two reasons: first, it ensures that at the beginning of their relationship with their prime brokers, leverage is set

accordingly. Second, when a hedge fund trades, it would like a prime broker that understands the nature of its trading activities.

A prime broker needs complete understanding of the hedge fund's style and trading strategy as well as working with a wide range of hedge funds.

- **Transparent capital introduction process** – The misconception in the financial industry is that a prime broker can raise capital for hedge funds. This misconception is being corrected by industry experts. In truth, prime brokers only introduce hedge funds to potential investors with the wherewithal and interest to invest in a particular hedge fund. If a prime broker were to raise capital for a hedge fund, the prime broker would be contravening mandated marketing restrictions.

- **Provision of a variety of solutions to leverage** – Hedge funds that use leverage would want a prime broker that can extend the required leverage. Therefore, it is essential that a prime broker has a variety of leverage products in their product range. These should include ordinary leverage and enhanced leverage. In a business terrain such as the hedge fund marketplace, where there are constant changes in regulation, a prime broker that understands these regulatory changes and can provide a number of different opportunities to hedge funds to achieve their leverage objectives, especially in the event of regulatory changes that could affect their current leverage, is desirable. Hedge funds would also want their prime broker to have a variety of methods to extend leverage to both their onshore and offshore funds.

- **Cash management capabilities** – In the current business environment, hedge funds have more cash on hand than in the past and would require dedicated cash management and fixed-rate financing facilities from their prime broker. Hedge funds would want a prime broker that has the expertise and bargaining power to achieve better returns for any cash holdings.

- **Efficient back-office function** – As the core of the prime brokerage offering is back-office, hedge funds would want a prime broker that has a demonstrable and experienced operations department. There should be evidence of an effortless dispatch of duties in the separate departments from cage[16] to margin and they should work seamlessly. The assessment of the prime brokerage back-office function should cover their ability to handle difficult situations or problems that extend beyond plain vanilla situations. The breadth of the range of activities of the back office should demonstrate the ability to resolve problems.

- **Strong global securities presence** – Hedge funds want a prime broker that can not only lend both stocks and bonds but one that also has a strong global presence. The prime broker should also have access to hard-to-borrow securities and be able to provide information on the state of the market and timely warnings about potential buy-ins.

---

16 A term used to describe the department of a prime brokerage firm that receives and distributes physical securities.

- **Provision of a range of mechanisms for trading** – Hedge funds want a prime broker that can provide them with multiple ways to trade. Different trading styles need different platforms, therefore hedge funds require a variety of electronic platforms for trading. Hedge funds that use a third-party or proprietary trading platform would want a prime broker that is connected or is able to connect to the hedge funds' preferred platform. Additionally, the prime broker should be able to offer both wholesale execution services and institutional coverage.

- **Strong technological capabilities** – A prime broker that is able to offer a variety of proprietary applications, including portfolio reporting and transparent reporting to the hedge funds' investors and shadow reporting,[17] is very desirable to any hedge fund. In addition, a variety of connectivity option such as FIX and dedicated circuits should be provided for these reports and applications. A veritable prime broker should also be connected to offshore administrator and middle-office providers.

- **Broad product capability** – A prime broker should be able to handle equity, fixed income, and derivative products including new issues, swaps and contracts-for-difference to meet the exacting requirements of their hedge fund clients. In addition, it should be able assist the hedge fund with repos and soft dollars. A prime broker should be able to meet reporting requirements that encompass all of the above products and be capable of providing margin across products. A sophisticated prime broker that is serious about the business of prime brokerage should demonstrate flexibility and capability across product lines. Hedge funds want a prime broker that has the depth and breadth to meet their future needs.

- **Full commitment to the prime brokerage business** – As hedge funds perceive prime brokerage as a business of consistency, integrity, reliability and experience and value their relationship with their prime broker, they would not be comfortable with appointing a prime broker that is in and out of prime brokerage every so often. Although it might be stating the obvious, a prime broker with a solid history and a track record of commitment to the prime brokerage business is more valuable to a hedge fund than one that has been sold a number of times or one that is treated as a sideline by its parent bank.

- **Back-office and front-office integration** – Hedge funds want a prime broker whose back-office technology is seamlessly integrated into front-office solutions, given that prime brokers have historically segmented their business along product lines, such as equities, fixed-income securities, commodities and foreign exchange, with different technology platforms and databases servicing each distinct segment. But nowadays hedge funds require prime brokers to seamless process their trades across multiple asset classes and products simultaneously.

---

17 Shadow reporting is a service which prime brokers offer to hedge funds that allows them to consolidate positions held by other prime brokers into one report.

- **Accesses to the firm** – Hedge funds perceive prime brokers as the window to the firm, i.e. the investment banks, to which they are affiliated. Hedge funds consider the capabilities of the entire organisation when choosing a prime broker.
- **Flexibility in decisions** – Hedge funds want a prime broker that is flexible in terms of its financing alternatives and reporting capabilities. They would want a prime broker that is able to adapt to its clients' individual requirements in these two essential areas, that is on the assumption that all regulatory requirements are met.

Legal Aspects of the Prime Broker–Hedge Fund Relationship

While the details of the legal relationship between a prime broker and its hedge fund client are outside the scope of this book, a brief discussion of the key documents that define and shape the legal relationship is necessary.

The documents to be discussed in this section include Request for Proposal (RFP), Prime Brokerage Agreement (PBA), Confidentiality Agreement, Service Level Agreement (SLA), Executing Broker Agreements, ISDAs and Side Letters.

Before discussing these documents, it is essential to gain an understanding of where the hedge fund–prime broker relationship begins. Whilst there are varying opinions, the definitive starting point is where the promoters of the hedge fund decide to start the fund. At this stage, a raft of activities is initiated including:

- the definition of the hedge fund strategy;
- the identification of markets and instruments;
- the engagement of the services of service providers;
- the drafting of the investor profiles.

It is also at this stage that the most important documents, including the Request for Proposal and the Prime Brokerage Agreement, are generated.

Given the increasing complexity of the prime broker–hedge fund relationship, prime brokers are no longer selected by referrals, on the basis of their ability to source securities or borrow in a certain jurisdiction, or other considerations discussed in the previous section. In addition, prime brokerage agreements are no longer signed on an "as is" basis and these days there are substantial negotiations involved in retaining a prime broker. Hedge funds have wised up to the need to select prime brokers through the RFP process and negotiate documents before they are signed.

It is without doubt that to ensure the success of the prime broker–hedge fund relationship, meaningful negotiations and dialogue are critical. The current structure of hedge funds would not be the way it is without the essential services that prime brokers provide to the hedge fund industry.

The definitions of the legal documents are as follows:

- **Request for Proposal** – The RFP is the document used to describe the hedge fund's requirements and to provide an outline of what a prime broker can bid for, and in the event of winning, negotiate by way of mandate, services, markets, products and costs. While there is no specific template for an RFP, the following list of features of the prime broker is included (please note that the list is not exhaustive):

  - detailed information about the prime broker, including its experience as a prime broker and regulatory history;
  - type of legal entity that the prime broker is;
  - types of transactions that can be supported and otherwise;
  - fees, costs and charges;
  - insurance coverage;
  - geographical scope, i.e. countries in which the prime broker operates;
  - current arrangements with executing brokers put forward.

  The prime broker, in turn, should respond to the RFP, needing clarification for the following among others:[18]

  - the exclusivity of the relationship;
  - the country restrictions on the instruments the hedge fund trades or intends to trade;
  - the prime broker's desire to have a dual role as the custodian or whether the hedge fund will be interested in using the prime broker's affiliated custodians;
  - the methods for custody of assets;
  - local country risks for netting, default, insolvency and/or bankruptcy;
  - limitation, or lack of, in the hypothecation of assets;[19]
  - the methods for calculating margin and the making of margin calls.

- **Confidentiality agreement** – Confidentiality is extremely important in the financial markets, and many contracting parties use confidentiality agreements to ensure that sensitive information disclosed by one party to another is kept secret. Hence, a confidentiality agreement can be defined as a document that by its terms allows two or more parties to share confidential information and to maintain the confidentiality of such information. Confidentiality agreements are ideally signed before the hedge fund issues the RFP and negotiates the Prime Brokerage Agreement (see below) with the candidate prime broker. This allays the fears of hedge funds that the RFP and related information is not misused or circulated by the candidate prime brokers. In most cases, the responsibility of signing the confidentiality agree-

18 There are other issues, but these depend on the individual prime broker's capabilities. Hence this list is not exhaustive.
19 The pledging of securities as collateral.

ment falls to the directors of the hedge fund. However, if the hedge fund has not been incorporated, the counsel to the hedge funds takes on this responsibility.

Every prime broker responding to an RFP should be made to sign an identical confidentiality agreement in partial fulfilment of the RFP process. It is essential that the confidentiality agreement should be of significant clarity and contain terms that can be enforced.

- ■ **Prime Brokerage Agreement** – This is a legal document which details the agreement under which the prime broker makes a range of services available to an entity, in this case a hedge fund. It can also be described as a document that lays out the legal relationship between the hedge fund and the prime broker. There are two basic types of PBAs (and further variations on each): the US model, which can be driven by US legal requirements and is used by US entities; and the international model that is used by non-US prime brokers.[20]

The PBA is signed by the directors of the hedge fund and the prime broker. Depending on the arrangement between the prime broker and the client, additional documents may need to be signed in conjunction with the PBA.

Contained in the PBA are legal issues, the majority of which are briefly described as follows (please note that this list of issues does not represent an exhaustive list as this legal aspect of the prime broker–hedge fund relationship is outside the scope of this book):

- ■ **How assets are to be held** – A number of factors determine the way that assets are held and these include the type of entity that the prime broker is, its structure and where it is affiliated.
- ■ **Margin** – This is an important aspect of the agreement and there should be a clear definition of what margin is and how it is to be calculated.
- ■ **Hypothecation** – The definition of the asset that the prime broker can hypothecate is equally important and must be clearly stated in the agreement.
- ■ **Use of excess cash** – It should be clearly defined how the hedge fund's excess cash will be handled by the prime broker.
- ■ **Security interest** – The charges over the hedge fund's assets in the portfolio of assets held should also be defined. Also essential is the declaration of whether the charge is fixed or floating.
- ■ **Termination** – The circumstances under which a hedge fund's prime brokerage account can be closed should be defined. According to legal experts, prime brokers prefer unilateral termination provisions that give them the right to close the prime brokerage for specific reasons or, in some cases, no reason at all.

20 Source: Breman B. (2007). "Hedge Funds and Prime Brokers". Risk Books.

- **Executing broker agreement** – This is an agreement that hedge fund managers enter into with their trading counterparts and their prime brokers. Hedge funds execute trades through executing broker (dealers) and these trades are given up to the prime broker for clearing. Executing broker agreements are essential because they provide a means by which trading and give-ups occur.
- **Service level agreement (SLA)** – This is a service contract where the level of service is formally defined. Prime brokers enter into SLAs with hedge funds as part of the requirements that hedge funds lay down for their service providers. An SLA provides a means for prime brokers to measure hedge fund performance and is usually signed by both prime broker and hedge fund to ensure that the terms of the agreement can be enforced. SLAs are also subject to regular reviews.

    SLAs have become more popular with the advent of hedge funds using multiple prime brokers.
- **Offering materials and verification notes** – Offering materials are the documents that are used to market shares of hedge funds. Also contained in the documents is the explicit statement of the important terms of the prime brokerage agreement as well as the summary information about the prime broker.

    There are requirements for the prime broker to sign verification notes. These notes are used to validate the statements in the offering materials and make certain that there is consistency in the disclosures in all documents.
- **ISDAs** – An ISDA (International Swap and Derivatives Association) Master Agreement is a contract between two parties (usually financial institutions) that outlines the basic rules under which the two parties will trade under the ISDA guidelines. This agreement allows counterparties to trade derivative instruments with terms and conditions that are of market standards.

    The conditions for negotiating ISDA agreements are outside the scope of this book, but it is useful to know that most hedge funds have at least an ISDA prepared as it is anticipated that trading of derivatives will become part of their activities at a given time, especially if they wish to hedge their positions.

    In practice, the negotiation of the ISDA schedule is started before the PBA is presented to directors of the hedge fund for sign-off.
- **Side letters** – Some hedge funds issue undisclosed side letters which offer enhanced liquidity and other preferential benefits to selected investors, to the potential detriment of other investors in the fund. These side letters are characterised by enforceable terms.

Regulators such as the UK's FSA and the US' SEC are increasingly concerned about the ramifications of the use of these side letters. Foremost among their concerns is the conflict of interest that could potentially harm the interests of investors.

A more detailed discussion on side letters is outside the scope of this book. However, it is worth noting that the existence of side letters in the hedge fund industry impacts on the hedge fund–prime broker relationship.

The Trading and Economic Factors Driving the Relationship

Paul Dentskevich
HSH Nordbank AG

This chapter discusses the trading and economic factors driving the relationship between prime brokers and their hedge fund clients

Paul Dentskevich (2007) Hedge Funds and Prime Brokers, Risk Books. Reproduced with Permission.

Introduction

When asked to identify the key factors that drive their relationship with their prime broker(s), hedge fund managers may respond with many possible answers. On the whole, managers go about their business primarily concerned with trading issues (and continued growth in AUM) and do not wish to become involved with "issues at the edge", such as why something cannot be done, why something went wrong, why did that particular trade fail or why can't I borrow that stock. Key employees of the manager – the fund manager(s), the trader, the administration liaison and distribution and marketing staff – desire an environment where their efforts can focus on the priorities of executing their strategies in the most efficient manner, increasing assets under management (AUM) and addressing investor queries smoothly and efficiently. The prime broker, in providing the needed funding, stock and cap intros, plus key risk management tools, is at the centre of nearly everything that the manager does.

The "Relationship" Side of the Trading and Economic Factors

During the life of a hedge fund, many factors will influence its relationship with its prime broker(s). These factors will wax and wane in importance and change or drop away, to be replaced by other issues.

Ultimately, economics is at the heart of the relationship. In the lead up to launch and in the early days of a hedge fund's life, securing assets under management sufficient to launch and to trade to start to deliver a respectable performance is the most pressing issue. The ability of the prime broker to introduce potential investors to the hedge fund and to secure initial investments helps set the tone for much that follows. Success may be measured not just from the volume/magnitude of investments but also from the correlation of claims made during the "courting" phase to launch and through the first year or two. Often, a relationship can be made, or soured, in the early days when claims of access to large numbers of potential investors eager to hear this hedge fund's story and invest does or does not materialise or leads to little or no investment. A related concern is a promise of seed capital from the prime broker itself that, in the course of the request for proposal (RFP) process and negotiations leading to the decision by the directors to retain that firm, comes in timely – or is a fraction of what was promised, is heavily conditioned, is delayed or does not come about.

Other factors that emerge at the beginning of the relationship are agreements to renegotiate fees during the first six months/one year, and a promise of fee breaks in return for a commitment by the hedge fund not to change prime brokers or to retain a second prime broker for a defined period. When the fund begins to grow and during or at the end of the first year, the parties would hold an "assessment meeting" and the "economics" of the relationship would become a discussion point.

It is at this point that the parties will start to focus on one of the "core" elements of the hedge fund–prime broker relationship – "profits vs service" – and possibly act on it for the first time. The future direction and fate of the relationship might be defined at this time. A prime broker that balances fees and profits with service will retain this and other hedge fund clients. Rigidity in fees, a large number of failed cap intros, DKs[21] trades, the quality of the advice and the efficiency with which ad hoc requests are satisfied may make or break the relationship.

Differences between Prime Brokerage Services

At present there is not a "one size fits all" approach to the services offered by prime brokers to the hedge fund industry at large. There are extensive differences between the prime brokerage services for equity-related, fixed income or credit-related hedge funds, and between prime brokers that service FX, commodity and futures-based funds.

Equity-related hedge funds are looking for easy financing of their trading activities, the ability to buy and sell stocks in an affordable manner. In its simplest form, financing is a floating rate line of credit (usually related to Libor); however, there are subtle variations on the theme. Some prime brokers offer gross pricing, which means that a hedge fund pays one rate for financing and receives a different, lower rate, for credit balances it maintains.

Other prime brokers offer net pricing, which means that credit balances are offset against debit balances before determining financing charges. Proponents of gross pricing argue that it is more transparent, and that those that offer net pricing will simply recoup any benefits received by charging higher stock loan fees. In reality, the important point is that the hedge fund directors must clearly understand the charging structure before signing. It is advisable to compare the charges of various prime brokers based on different scenarios, e.g. net long, net short, to determine the most favourable charging structure.

Other features such as auto-borrow make life easy, although some versions of this are not quite automatic. This leads to delays in getting stock and impacts trading. Quite often it is in times of market dislocation or excessive volatility that issues concerning stock borrowing arise. The supply of "easy to borrow" stocks may slow or dry, leading to delays in settlement or DK'd trades. Another issue may be that fund managers do not check the list as thoroughly as they might, or not at all (thinking that there have not been changes to the list), and trade, to learn that stock cannot be timely delivered or to see that trades fail. Depending on the terms of the PBA, prime brokers may have an absolute right to DK trades without notice or for no reason, and a drying up of their supply of

---

21 An expression for an out trade that is used when there is a discrepancy in the details of a trade. In this kind of trade, one of the counterparties "doesn't know (DK) the trade". This counterparty either lacks information or has received inaccurate trading instructions.

stock or a surge in borrowing a particular position might cause them strains that, in turn, impact trading and result in an intraday change to the "easy to borrow" list.

Fixed income prime brokerage formerly took the form of simply providing custodial services and financing obtained in the repo market. Generally, the prime broker would have an expectation that the majority of the hedge fund's repo trading would be through it, and the relationship would become strained when this was not the case. An increasing number of houses offer a fixed income equivalent to the services they offer to equity hedge funds.

Prime brokers are also offering cash management, funding and FX services. The advent of intermediation has simplified many aspects of the functioning of the credit derivatives market: the costs can be quite significant and leave funds with a decision to either resource themselves or pay for the convenience.

Economics

As noted above, numerous economic factors have a direct influence on the relationship. What follows is a discussion of a few of the more prominent examples that may be provided by the prime broker and that shape the hedge fund's portfolio and returns – that may lead to gains and increased fees or even result in the creation of friction in the relationship. This list is by no means exhaustive, but helps to illustrate how certain economic factors influence the relationship, for the better and for the worse.

Trading Equities vs CFDs

One of the hot topics in the UK is the question of whether to buy equities, CFDs or total return swaps. The cost of buying equities vs CFDs or swaps is more than just an issue of financing. In the UK, cash purchases of cash equities by investors (not intermediaries) attract stamp duty, currently 50 bp. The more a hedge fund buys UK equities, the more stamp duty it pays and the more performance is affected. Using derivatives, total return swaps or CFDs to replicate the economic exposure of equities helps a hedge fund reduce its purchasing costs by eliminating the need to pay stamp duty. (The prime broker or executing broker would not be liable for stamp duty to the extent that it acquired the underlying position as an intermediary.) It is an attractive proposition to a hedge fund. It does, however, require the implementation of special arrangements and documentation by which the hedge fund's executing broker sells the derivative to the hedge fund while the prime broker or the executing broker (not the hedge fund) achieves the underlying equity to hedge its exposure. It also needs to be done in a manner that would not result in HMR&C taking the position that the procedure employed resulted in avoidance or evasion, and assessing tax, interest or penalties. Considerable care needs to be taken in drawing up the documentation and implementing the procedures. The hedge fund should avoid any steps that might result in the prime broker or the executing broker putting any underlying equity back to the hedge fund.

It is worth adding a cautionary note about Ireland where the Office of Revenue Commissioners considered looking to prevent such types of arrangement. No action was taken, out of a desire to avoid having Irish equities become less competitive than UK stocks.

UK managers of hedge funds have made extensive use of CFDs. Estimates of the use of hedge funds trading CFDs have ranged as high as 50% of the market for this instrument in London. Trading CFDs may be economically sound, but may also lead to issues for managers that run long and long-short funds that each trade CFDs (the long only fund must be properly empowered to be able to trade these instruments at all). Trading CFDs for both long and long-short funds might result in issues under UK FSA rules (conflicts of interest, allocations), potential HMR&C matters and, possibly, concerns that investors are not being treated equally.

Electronic Trading Platforms

An integrated trading platform that permits automated trading or facilitates straight-through processing is a powerful, efficient tool. Such a system generates significant cost savings and adds value, provided it has sufficient operational support. The degree to which prime brokers can offer these services varies, but those who do certainly give hedge funds a real "leg up".[22] Such a system not only helps a hedge fund gain good access to markets but it leads to greater efficiencies in execution and risk management.

It is essential when considering an integrated trading platform, or any software or back-office platform, for the manager to bench-test the product, negotiate the documentation carefully, ensure compatibility with current (and proposed) systems (both in-house and for interfaces with systems of other service providers), negotiate costs, consult with other service providers (in particular, the administrator and providers of risk management software) and obtain references from current users. Decisions should not be made based on presentation material, which quite often focuses on "bells and whistles", but on thorough due diligence. The directors of the hedge fund should have a demonstration, interview the purveyor and, in the proper discharge of their oversight responsibilities, have a say in cost and functionality issues. Hedge funds considering such a system should obtain examples of reports that the system generates (cash forecast ladders, FX exposures), and speak to other funds that use the system to confirm reliability and the usefulness of the features that attracted the manager in the first place.

One should examine carefully the calculations that the system is reputed to make; for example, what are the parameters used in calculating beta, can they be reconciled, how is credit and interest rate DV01 calculated, how are derivatives handled, etc? Whilst this can be a tedious process, it avoids the strains that

22 See "Citigroup unveils new prime brokerage platform", MarketWatch Weekend Edition, Dow Jones, 2 August 2006, available at www.marketwatch.com/News/Story/9CrbKW296m Fr9n8npZ5BxNg?siteid_mktw&dist_TNMostMailed.

may arise such as system breakdowns, incompatibility, less than promised functionality, errors and so on. A significant issue is the length of time required to implement updates or to fix problems. In such an event, if trades are DK'd or delays arise, it may not be possible to recover losses. Far worse is the spectre of having to trade round a platform with reduced functionality or to take it out completely.

Structured Products

The topic of structured products raises many issues, economic and non-economic. It is the readiness or pro-activeness of the prime broker to offer to fund, structure or engage in this activity with the hedge fund that can further, or harm, the relationship. Some prime brokers perpetually offer structures to their hedge fund clients. Not all of these deals are appropriate, made at the right time or are cost-effective. If they are done in the right way at the right time, they can provide a real benefit to the fund. Continuous dialogue and education helps to generate the flow of ideas, some of which might be quite useful. Quite often, total return swaps will enable hedge funds to gain economic exposures in companies where to acquire the equities would result in having to disclose holdings to the relevant authority. Similarly, using derivatives to avoid disclosure may result in other issues and might, in certain jurisdictions, kick off a disclosure obligation – such as in the UK where the Takeover Code now requires the disclosure of certain derivative positions in companies involved in takeovers.

Another "structured product" that is gaining favour in the fixed income world is the extended repo facility. These enable the hedge fund to closely control their funding and leverage. Extended repo facilities are long dated repos where the essential terms are negotiated and agreed at the time of trade: liquidity, haircut rates, and other material terms. Some of these instruments can be extremely deep and have significant maturities. The beauty of these structures is that the hedge fund can manage its collateral on a portfolio basis, rather than managing a portfolio of repos. "Swapping" stocks in and out of such a structure may take place without having to worry about early calls or the risk of having to finance open positions. In general, such a facility is attractive where the hedge fund controls activity and the prime broker does not have the right to call an issue. It should be noted that this facility might be obtained not just from the prime broker, but also from other counterparties.

Tax-efficient Structures

The prime broker can play a pivotal role in the creation of tax-efficient structures. Invariably, there is a wealth of expertise available in the prime broker and in its affiliates in the jurisdictions where the hedge fund trades. It is, however, axiomatic that different prime brokers have different areas of strength. The efficient execution of a deal quite often depends on local information and expertise. A prime broker who not only understands local requirements and idiosyncrasies, but also the needs of the hedge fund, can bring added value – translated, often, into increased performance, lower costs and better fees.

Dividend Enhancements

An example of a simple, effective tax-efficient strategy is dividend enhancements. Essentially, the hedge fund lends its stock to a firm or institution in a local market for a defined period (usually when the stock goes ex-dividend) and receives a better tax treatment when the dividend is paid. Typically, the benefit is shared among the arranger, the fund and the borrower. These strategies have been around for a long time, but as tax regimes converge, the benefit from such strategies may slowly decline.

Rehypothecation

Rehypothecation is an item that shapes the relationship but is rarely discussed. For the prime broker, the assets in the portfolio that it holds, and over which it has a security interest, provide a readily available source of securities and other instruments that it may lend and for which it pays little or nothing, and for which it may earn a profit. The extent to which prime brokers can rehypothecate is dictated by legal requirements imposed on the prime broker, the PBA and the offering materials, and is influenced by lending rates, the quality of the portfolio, market conditions, the nature of the security interest over the portfolio and the liabilities of the hedge fund. In the USA, there are rules governing the extent to which a prime broker can rehypothecate (140%, see related discussions in Chapters 2 and 3). In Europe there is no such limit, and the range can be anywhere from 100% to full access to the long side of the book. The appetite of the directors to permit a prime broker to leverage the portfolio solely to its pecuniary advantage tempers hypothecation. Directors may wish to impose limits on prime broker hypothecation but doing so in an aggressive manner might result in higher fees or other "roadblocks" being activated or implemented.

Concerns about hypothecation do arise when the prime broker hypothecates uncharged positions, where cash is returned to the portfolio rather than "equivalent securities", and when the directors challenge the profits made by the prime broker as excessive. Rehypothecation increases the hedge fund's exposure to the prime broker. It is when these issues arise or when the hedge fund experiences distress that the real impact is felt. Thus, there must be a constant dialogue between the manager, directors and prime broker to ensure that all aspects of hypothecation are understood, that clear provisions to govern this are in place and that if the directors require changes, they may be implemented with minimum fuss and expense.

Prime Brokerage Costs

The relationship with the prime broker is robust and delicate. The question of costs is always a subject of discussion and, unless controlled, a point of contention. The query is whether the costs should be "what we should actually pay" or be the subject of a "cost-cutting" exercise. Looking at the bottom line figure can give a hedge fund comfort, but it can also give a hedge fund cause for concern. While using a prime broker yields operational efficiencies that outweigh the costs of unbundled prime brokerage services, a thorough analysis can reveal the true costs a hedge fund pays. One must measure, for example, the costs of dealing away and give-ups against the achieved price for dealing solely through the prime broker, or the costs of the manager handling its own borrowing and lending. An obvious candidate would be the rates achieved on foreign exchange transactions achieved by dealing away, e.g. FX trading.

Single vs Multiple Prime Brokers

In the early stages of a hedge fund's life there is a need to achieve simplicity and one-stop shopping. A prime broker, as we have seen, can offer multiple services, all of which contribute to enhanced, cost-effective services and a successful relationship. As hedge funds grow they achieve growth and stature, become sophisticated in both trading and portfolio composition, and require increasingly sophisticated tools to trade and measure risk and performance, but need to control costs. It is at this point that a review of the services offered by prime brokers takes place, whether or not at the request of the directors, and when it might be found that these may be impediments to growth, flexibility and other considerations.

Adding a second prime broker at this time, or even earlier, can give the hedge fund flexibility in achieving its needs, and also a degree of leverage in terms of its relationship with its prime brokers. It may also achieve the need of giving the hedge fund a prime broker in a geographical or product market into which the hedge fund wishes to enter. For the prime broker, the risk of losing a client and associated revenue can sometimes lead to increased "flexibility" which may translate into better services and lower costs.

Funds with large AUMs seek to diversify their counterparty risk. Global hedge funds seek to gain the best access to their target markets. Having multiple prime brokers may help the hedge fund achieve its goals. It is wise to maximise all of the means at one's disposal to achieve efficient trading, maximise returns and control costs.

There are, however, downsides to having multiple prime brokers. One potential downside of running multiple prime brokers arises from having a fund's positions distributed around the market, which may make risk control and consolidation difficult if the right systems and processes are not in place.

Leverage

One of the most essential tools available to a hedge fund is the ability to leverage. Leverage can be achieved in many ways. Leverage involves the borrowing of funds and the investing of those borrowed funds in other assets. The borrowing is usually collateralised over existing assets. The new assets, in turn, may be used to raise more cash that, in turn, may be used to purchase more assets. In theory, but not in practice, this can go on ad infinitum. The counterparty providing the lending will, without exception, impose a haircut and lend less than the present value of the collateral, and levy a charge in the process. The inherent inefficiencies limit the absolute number of times that the hedge fund can repeat this trade.[23]

One of the essentials of any prime brokerage service is providing leverage. This has long been the norm in the equity long/short world, and is a feature of fixed income funds. Traditionally, fixed income funds have looked to the highly efficient repo market (not necessarily facing the prime broker) to secure their leverage as opposed to long/short equity hedge funds who source leverage from their prime broker.

The advantage of using the prime broker is that it can significantly reduce operational overheads. There is a cost for this, however, and that is the ceding of control over the portfolio. Letting the prime broker source leverage may put the hedge fund in a more exposed position with respect to credit exposure. Often, PBAs do not afford as much protection to the fund's assets as would, for example, a GMRA when executed with a third party.

Intermediation

Potentially one of the most time-consuming and heavily resourced activities for a hedge fund (alone or with an administrator) can be the confirmation and settlement of derivatives, especially CDSs. (A CDS may be likened to the buying or selling of protection/insurance on the creditworthiness of an issuer.) While the market has moved a long way towards standardisation, there are still many issues to be resolved, particularly if a hedge fund has several ISDA counterparties. The use of multiple counterparties can also lead to inefficient uses of capital, since invariably each transaction will have some form of collateralisation. Conversely, there may be benefits where there are numerous transactions that, if netted, might well lead to some benefits in the form of reduced costs.

Within a single counterparty, if the hedge fund has a soundly negotiated, balanced ISDA, one may expect to use cross-product netting (where collateral requirements from long and short obligations can be offset).

If derivatives are to be used, effective ISDA negotiation should be a priority. Hedge funds, especially young/small funds, will accept terms offered to them in an effort to secure a relationship and achieve the ability to transact with a particular counterparty – dealing outweighs negotiation. In such a case, the new hedge fund is subject to provisions that are not within the market standards for large, mature hedge funds. Such terms, including NAV decline triggers,

---

23 For example, a fund holding €1 borrows €1, giving it €2 to invest. If the investment pays off, the fund's €2 would become €4 that, after the repayment of the €1 loan, would leave the fund with €3 and a return of 200%, vs 100% if the fund did not borrow (or leverage) with its original €1. The risk, of course, is that the markets turn against the fund and the €2 investment shrinks to, say, 50 cents. You then can cash out at 50 cents, but have to repay the €1 borrowed, leaving the fund with nothing or, if the decline is severe or the leverage is great, a loss.

key person losses, late delivery of documents, and so on, as well as additional termination events, low additional cross-termination amounts and onerous events of default, leave a new fund in a precarious position should anything go wrong – including market declines, large redemptions and so on. Promises to renegotiate terms in such instances or to forego exercising provisions are more often than not reduced to writing.

There are ways in which this can be avoided. The first is to negotiate to achieve the same terms across all counterparties. This can be a timely and costly process. However, balancing this is the spectre of uneven ISDA provisions that increase operational and credit risk. Alternatively, a hedge fund can look to intermediation. Intermediation is essentially a "give-up agreement" where the hedge fund can deal with any counterparty with whom it has an ISDA in place, which trade is then given up to the prime broker so that the fund is left facing the prime broker. This introduces increased credit exposure to the prime broker, but at the same time the hedge fund benefits from reduced collateralisation due to the netting of trades. The overhead is further reduced since in executing the intermediation, the prime broker will undoubtedly employ the checks and balances that would be left with the hedge fund if it maintained its deals with its trade counterparts.

It should be noted that it is still essential to have and to trade under ISDAs in place with the hedge fund's other counterparties. In this case, existence of cross-default clauses and NAV decline triggers, unequal or evened out across the hedge fund's documentation, can still put the fund in a position of "discomfort".

The introduction of intermediation has meant a great deal to many hedge funds, simplifying their derivative (especially CDS) trading activity and helping control costs. Prime brokers have also benefited due to increased revenues. Offering an integrated trading platform at an early stage helps not only to ensure continued trade flow and activity but also to recoup costs.

Conclusion

Prime brokerage allows hedge funds to maximise their credit relationships and activities while improving efficiency. In addition, prime brokerage streamlines the credit and documentation process, given that the hedge fund is subject to one internal credit review and executes one master trading agreement and credit support annex with the prime broker, rather than many agreements with multiple dealers. An effective PBA provides for the more efficient use of collateral for margin relationships. Margin positions can be netted as the hedge fund needs to manage one credit relationship to achieve trading relationships with many counterparties. In addition, the client is able to access pricing and liquidity from a greater number of dealers and potentially to expand the range of its activities.

There are many factors that drive the hedge fund–prime broker relationship. Many are positive, but negative experiences leave a lasting taint on the relationship and may even serve to dissuade new hedge funds from using a particular prime broker. What are the avoidable issues? Promises to renegotiate or to forebear using clauses that are postponed. Promises to introduce prospects that lead to little or no investment. Automated systems that do not operate, that do not provide promised or required functionality or that are not bug-free. Hastily withdrawn, or no, seed capital. DK'd trades or misbookings. Non-payment of interest on balances, over-collateralisation of derivative and FX transactions, unilateral amendments to PBAs or other documents without providing the appropriate or advance notification. Overcharging, dramatically increased fees or a lack of transparency in charging. A reluctance to process give-ups. Fails to deliver when there is inventory.

Quite often it falls on the administrator to address and rectify the problems, but serious issues require the attention of the individual fund managers in the manager itself, or even the directors. This saps resources and undoubtedly affects performance.

Ultimately, and for final consideration, is the query whether it really matters how much a hedge fund pays a prime broker, as long as the hedge fund receives good performance, the NAV per share increases and investors and service providers are happy. Happiness and indifference to fees do not always go hand in hand. Costs and fees, key planks in the economic fabric of the hedge fund–prime broker relationship, will always play a part and will have an impact on the hedge fund's trading. Ultimately, the goals of every investor, and of the hedge fund, the prime broker and the directors, are to limit exposure and risk, to make money and to keep expenses under control. These in turn lead to sound economics and a healthy trading relationship. Achieve a healthy balance and all parties involved realise a win-win. Lose the balance and the relationship may become soured, or fall apart. In the end, as there will always be hedge funds and prime brokers, there will always be trading and economics to help share this relationship – for the sake of the markets and investors, for the better.

The Business Environment

This chapter gives an overview of the business environment in which prime brokers operate. This includes profiles of allied organisations such as regulators, exchanges and service providers.

Introduction

The business environment in prime brokerage is shaped by factors similar to those that shape both the hedge fund and investment banking industries. These environmental factors impact on the ability of prime brokers to deliver the plethora of services they offer to hedge funds.

Traditional environmental factors such as interest rates, exchange rates, regulations and technological advancements that affect the parent investment banks of most prime brokers will naturally impact on the ability of the prime broker to operate.

The interaction between prime brokers and the business environment is unique in the sense that they are service providers that service a very narrow market, i.e. the hedge fund marketplace, and therefore their fortunes are tied to the interaction of hedge funds with the business environment, especially the regulatory environment.

Figure 5.1 The Prime Broker's business environment

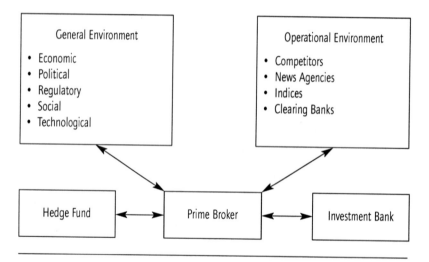

The Environmental Factors affecting Prime Brokers

Political

The political environmental factors are centred around the recent regulations that impact on the activities of both hedge funds and investment banks. Notable among them are the Markets in Financial Instruments Directive (MiFID), the Sarbanes-Oxley Act of 2002 (SOX), the Basel II Accord and Undertakings for Collective Investment in Transferable Securities (UCITS III).

Industry experts opine that regulatory issues are generally perceived as enabling as opposed to restricting and the prime brokerage model is perceived as one that evolves to meet the changing regulatory environment.

There follows a brief description of these regulations.

MiFID

The main objective of MiFID is to help issuers of securities and investors by opening up markets and cutting the costs of securities trading. It is a groundbreaking piece of legislation that experts believe will transform the landscape for the trading of securities and introduce competition and efficiency.

MiFID provides consumer protection in the investment industry by promoting a competitive environment, with investors being given the right to ask investment firms to provide evidence to show that they have given the investors what they promised. This is referred to as "best execution". The best execution requirement is an important component of these investor protection standards.

MiFID imposes several obligations on investment firms such as hedge fund management firms to fulfil its requirement of best execution by taking all reasonable steps to obtain the best possible result for the execution of client orders, taking into account price, costs, speed, likelihood of execution and settlement, size, nature or any other consideration relevant to the execution of the order.

SOX

This is legislation that requires all public companies to submit an annual assessment of the effectiveness of their internal financial auditing controls to the Securities and Exchange Commission (SEC). There are 11 sections of the Sarbanes-Oxley Act, including sections 302, 401, 404 and 802. Section 404 – management of internal control – requires that financial reports must include an Internal Control Report stating that management is responsible for an "adequate" internal control structure. This is the most difficult section of the Act to comply with.

Non-compliance and submission of inaccurate certification could lead to a fine of $1 million and 10 years' imprisonment, even if committed in error.

Basel II

This is the second of the Basel accords, which are recommendations on banking laws and regulations issued by the Basel Committee on Banking Supervision. The main aim of Basel II is to create an international standard that industry regulators can use when formulating regulations regarding capital adequacy that are required to guard against the types of financial and operational risk that banks face.

The Basel II framework consists of three "pillars":

- Pillar 1 sets out the minimum capital requirements that firms will be required to meet to cover credit, market and operational risk.
- The rules under Pillar 2 create a new supervisory review process. This requires financial institutions to have their own internal processes to assess

their capital needs and appoint supervisors to evaluate an institution's overall risk profile, to ensure that they hold adequate capital.

■ The aim of Pillar 3 is to improve market discipline by requiring firms to publish certain details of their risks, capital and risk management.

UCITS III

This is the third version of the original directive adopted in 1985 to allow for open-ended funds investing in transferable securities to be subject to the same regulation in every Member State in Europe. It consists of the following two directives:

1. The Management Directive that seeks to give management companies a "European passport" to operate throughout the EU and widens the activities which they are allowed to undertake.
2. The Product Directive that has the objective of removing barriers to the cross-border marketing of units of collective investment funds by allowing funds to invest in a wider range of financial instruments. Under the new Directive, it is possible to establish derivatives funds, index-tracking funds and funds of funds as UCITS.

Economic

The economic factors in the business environment that will impact on the operations of prime brokers include:

■ **Interest rates** – Movements in interest rates can impact on the securities lending, fixed income servicing aspect of the prime brokerage business. Demands for fixed income securities are higher as interest rates rise given the more favourable yield that investors can get from investing in fixed income. As a consequence, prime brokers get to support more fixed income transactions.

With regard to securities lending, prime brokers will generate more revenue from the securities loaned out to their clients.

■ **Exchange rates** – Hedge fund clients of prime brokers that are active in the currency space are impacted by movements in the exchange rates. The trading activities of these types of fund manager will determine the level of service they require with respect to clearing and settlement. In addition, movements in exchange rates are a determinant in the demand for international securities, thus an increase in the demand for these securities and a resultant demand for prime brokerage services from hedge fund managers will impact on the revenue stream of prime brokers.

■ **Stock market** – Activities in the stock markets such as initial price offerings (IPOs), rights issues, mergers and acquisitions are a boon to prime brokers as they increase the trading activities of their hedge fund clients in the equities space.

Social

The social environment has minimal impact on prime brokers as they mostly service corporate entities, especially hedge funds. But hedge funds are patronised by both private and institutional investors and the attitude of private investors towards hedge fund investing could impact on the fortunes of hedge fund managers. For instance, a number of hedge funds went bust during the credit crunch due to their exposure to the US sub-prime crisis. These events could put potential investors off hedge fund investing and thus reduce the volume of business that prime brokers get from hedge funds. A typical example, according to the Sunday Times, is JWM Partners, the latest venture by one of the promoters of the infamous Long-Term Capital Management company, which in 1998 lost $4.6 billion and helped to plunge the global financial market into crisis. It is reported that its biggest fund, a bond portfolio, had fallen by 26% as of May 2008 and another fund by 12%.[24]

Experts have long opined that even the smartest of hedge fund managers cannot control events such as the credit crunch that could lead to the collapse of their hedge funds.

Legal

As relationships between prime brokers, clients and the executing dealers that clients often execute trades with are governed by agreements such as prime brokerage agreements, changes in the relevant laws could impact on the way these entities interact with each other with respect to structuring the terms of these agreements.

According to legal experts, the prime brokerage agreement between a prime broker and, say, a hedge fund client in a particular jurisdiction would not specify the choice of law and forum. In practice, the law of the country or continent where the contract was drawn up will be applicable to the interpretation of the contracts as well as in litigation.

Technological

Advances in technology can impact on how prime brokers service their clients, especially in clearing and settlement. Innovations in order management, electronic trading platforms and messaging technology can provide a prime broker with competitive advantage in an age where hedge funds have chosen to engage the services of more than one prime broker. For instance, hedge funds execute trades with executing dealers and have to communicate details of the trade to the prime broker in a timely manner. Advances in messaging protocols such as FIX can ensure that the trade information is transmitted quickly, reducing the time taken to settle the trade. Early adopters of new technology can have a competitive edge at least until the time that competitors follow suit.

---

24 Rush, D. (25 May 2008) "Echoes of the Past: LTCM Meriwether in Trouble Again", The Sunday Times Special Report.

The Global Custodian Prime Brokerage Survey[25]

If there is one lesson to be learned from the annual *Global Custodian* survey of how hedge funds rate the quality of the services of the prime brokers, it is that no two prime brokers are alike. The aptitude of both prime brokers and the trade press to reduce the survey findings to a league table (see Table 5.1), purporting to the show the best and worst prime brokers, obscures the significant differences between firms in size and ownership structure, geographic coverage, services provided, core strengths, and target markets.

Goldman Sachs and Morgan Stanley have significantly larger client bases than any other prime brokers. Credit Suisse has an explicit focus on the largest funds with institutional backing, while Bank of America (acquired in 2008 by BNP Paribas) specialised in smaller funds in the US domestic market. Newedge specialises in CTAs, and earns as much from investors as fund managers. Barclays Capital, BNP Paribas, Citi, Deutsche Bank and Merrill Lynch specialise in so-called synthetic prime brokerage, in which clients invest, finance and hedge using OTC derivatives.

Beyond the major global firms active in all three major regions – Asia, Europe and North America – lies a long tail of smaller broker-dealers and investment banks active in one or two countries or a handful of markets. The *Global Custodian* survey monitors some sizeable second-tier investment banks in the United States (such as Jefferies & Company and Shoreline) but also nearly a dozen "mini" prime brokers. In Canada, the investment banking arm of all the major banks - BMO Capital Markets, NBCN, RBC Capital Markets, Scotia Capital TD Securities – all service Canadian hedge funds.

As the hedge fund industry grows, it can accommodate more providers, and competition is intensifying. One fund manager (Fidelity) participates in the *Global Custodian* survey. The global custodian banks, which have long acted as agents in the lending and financing of institutional securities portfolios, are following traditional fund management clients into prime brokerage-style services. JPMorgan Chase has now added an equity finance house (Bear Stearns) to its strengths in synthetic financing, securities financing and custody. BNY Mellon is developing a prime brokerage business via its Pershing broker-dealer clearing arm.

New entrants are routinely dismissed as late and unrealistic, but every year sees firms participating in the *Global Custodian* survey for the first time, or lifting their exposure and performance to a new level. The reluctance of some established firms to service smaller and start-up funds – the *Global Custodian* survey finds virtually no prime broker excels at capital introductions – has created room for smaller broker-dealers to service them instead. Simultaneously, the reluctance of hedge fund managers to deal with one provider, and their desire to tap specialist skills, means no provider owns all of the business of all

---

25 Contributed by Dominic Hobson of Global Custodian.

of its clients any more.

Corporate activity following changes of strategy creates further opportunities for once-marginal providers to add scale quickly. Bear Stearns was rescued by JPMorgan Chase, but Bank of America sold its prime brokerage to BNP Paribas. Newedge, launched in January 2008, was created by a merger of the brokerage arms of Calyon (the investment banking division of Crédit Agricole) and Fimat (the investment banking division of Société Générale). As the *Global Custodian* survey shows, prime brokerage is an industry in which there is an established hierarchy, but change is constant, and the large differences between providers are important for hedge fund managers to understand.

Table 5.1 The Global Prime Brokers

Prime Broker	Global Weighted Average Score
1. Deutsche Bank	5.95
2. Merrill Lynch	5.90
3=. Bear Stearns (now JPMorgan Chase)	5.88
3=. Morgan Stanley	5.88
5=. Lehman Brothers	5.85
5=. UBS	5.85
7. Credit Suisse Prime Services	5.83
8. Citi Prime Services	5.82
9. Goldman Sachs	5.62
10. Barclays Capital	5.60

Source: Global Custodian Prime Brokerage Survey 2008

Allied Industries

Regulators
Financial Services Authority (FSA)

The Financial Services Authority (FSA) is an independent non-departmental public and quasi-judicial body that regulates the financial services industry in the United Kingdom. Its main office is based in Canary Wharf, London, with another office in Edinburgh. When acting as the competent authority for the listing of shares on a stock exchange, it is referred to as the UK Listing Authority (UKLA) and maintains the Official List.

The FSA's main role in the prime brokerage industry is to regulate the firms as well as reduce financial crime. Prime brokers have to comply with sets of regulations that govern the financial industry and have a requirement to report their activities to the FSA.

Bank of England
The Bank of England is the central bank of the United Kingdom and has two core purposes – monetary stability and financial stability. The bank has the leg-

islative responsibility through the Monetary Policy Committee to set the UK's official interest rate and is also responsible for the issuing of banknotes. Apart from the monetary and financial stability roles, the bank works closely with financial markets and institutions to collate and publish monetary and banking statistics.

The Bank of England was established in 1694 to be the UK government's bank and since the late 18th century has been the bank to the banking system. It is based in Threadneedle Street in the heart of London's "square mile" and is sometimes referred to as the "Old Lady" of Threadneedle Street.

ECB

The European Central Bank (ECB) is the central bank for Europe's single currency, the euro. The ECB's main task is to maintain the euro's purchasing power and thus price stability in the euro area. The euro area comprises the 13 European Union countries that have introduced the euro since 1999.

Since 1 January 1999, the ECB has been responsible for conducting monetary policy for the euro area – the world's largest economy after the United States.

The euro area came into being when responsibility for monetary policy was transferred from the national central banks of 11 EU Member States to the ECB in January 1999. Greece joined in 2001, followed by Slovenia, the 13th member, in 2007. The creation of the euro area and a new supranational institution, the ECB, was a milestone in a long and complex process of European integration.

The ECB headquarters is in Frankfurt am Main, Germany.

Committee of European Securities Regulators

The Committee for European Securities Regulators (CESR) is an independent Committee of European Securities Regulators. Headquartered in Paris, France, the role of CESR is to:

- **improve coordination among securities regulators**: this is achieved by developing effective operational network mechanisms to enhance day-to-day consistent supervision and enforcement of the Single Market for financial services;
- **act as an advisory group to assist the EU Commission**: in particular in its preparation of draft implementing measures of EU framework directives in the field of securities;
- work to ensure more consistent and timely day-to-day implementation of community legislation in the Member States.

In June 2002, CESR established the Market Participants Consultative Panel. The role of the Panel is to:

- assist CESR in the definition of priorities and work programmes;
- provide comments on the way in which CESR is exercising its role and, in

particular, implementing its Public Statement of Consultation Practices;
- alert CESR on regulatory inconsistencies in the Single Market, and identify and suggest areas where CESR should undertake further work to improve supervisory co-ordination;
- inform CESR on major developments in financial markets and identify new elements for preliminary discussion by CESR.

Also, in 2003, CESR established the Review Panel to fulfil the task of securing more effective cooperation between national supervisory authorities, carrying out peer reviews and promoting best practice.

Securities and Exchange Commission (SEC)

The US Securities and Exchange Commission (SEC) is a United States government agency having primary responsibility for enforcing the federal securities laws and regulating the securities industry/stock market. The mission of the SEC is to protect investors, maintain fair, orderly and efficient markets, and facilitate capital formation.

The SEC oversees the key participants in the securities world, including securities exchanges, securities brokers and dealers, and investment advisers. In fulfilling this objective, the SEC is concerned primarily with promoting the disclosure of important market-related information, maintaining fair dealing and protecting against fraud. It is also currently responsible for administering six major laws that govern the securities industry. They are: the Securities Act of 1933, the Securities Exchange Act of 1934, the Trust Indenture Act of 1939, the Investment Company Act of 1940, the Investment Advisers Act of 1940 and, most recently, the Sarbanes-Oxley Act of 2002.

The SEC was formed in 1934 and its headquarters is in Washington DC. It employs 3,800 staff in its headquarters and 11 regional offices throughout the United States.

Exchanges
London Stock Exchange

The London Stock Exchange (LSE) based in London, United Kingdom, is one of the world's oldest stock exchanges and possibly one of the most international of all the world's stock exchanges, with 3,287[26] companies from over 60[27] countries admitted to trading on its markets.

The London Stock Exchange started life in the coffee houses of 17th-century London and grew to what is today one of the City of London's most important financial institutions.

Companies around the world that need to raise the capital needed for growth have a choice of four primary markets offered by the LSE:

---

26   As of November 2007.

27   Ibid.

- Main Market – a listing and trading environment for investors and companies;
- AIM – equities market for small capitalisation listings;
- Professional Securities Market – dedicated to listings of companies that raise capital through the issue of specialist securities, such as debt, convertibles and depositary receipts, to professional or institutional investors;
- Specialist Fund Market – regulated market for specialist investment funds, targeting institutional, professional and highly knowledgeable investors.

In 2007, the London Stock Exchange merged with Borsa Italiana, Italy's main stock exchange, creating what is perceived in the financial markets as Europe's leading equity platform.

NYSE Euronext

NYSE Euronext, the holding company created by the combination of NYSE Group Inc. and Euronext N.V., operates a liquid exchange group and offers an array of financial products and services.

The company is made up of four divisions:

- **New York Stock Exchange** – probably the largest equities marketplace in the world, with global market value of approximately $27.1 trillion, as of 31 December 2007;
- **Euronext** – pan-European stock exchange based in Paris and with subsidiaries in Belgium, France, Netherlands, Portugal and the United Kingdom;
- **NYSE Arca** – a fully electronic stock exchange that provides an open and fair market for emerging companies to expand;
- **Euronext.liffe** – a derivative exchange formed as a result of the takeover of the then London International Financial Futures and Options Exchange (LIFFE);
- **Powernext** – a European energy exchange, providing an electronic market similar to a stock market, for the trading of energy futures contracts and derivatives in Europe.

NYSE Euronext is a major force in the listings, trading in cash equities, equity and interest rate derivatives, bonds and the distribution of market data.

The following is a list of major NYSE Euronext locations:

- Brussels, Belgium – Euronext Brussels
- Paris, France – Euronext Paris
- Amsterdam, Netherlands – Euronext Amsterdam
- Lisbon, Portugal – Euronext Lisbon
- London, United Kingdom – Euronext.liffe
- Chicago, United States of America – NYSE Arca (formerly Archipelago)
- New York, United States of America – NYSE, Headquarters
- New York, United States of America – AMEX (to be relocated to NYSE headquarters)
- San Francisco, United States of America – NYSE Arca (formerly Pacific

Exchange)

NASDAQ

The NASDAQ, which stands for National Association of Securities Dealers Automated Quotient, is an electronic screen-based equity securities trading market in the United States. It is headquartered in New York City, USA.

The history of NASDAQ dates back to February 1971 when it became the world's first electronic stock market. As of March 2008, it lists approximately 3,100 companies and, on average, trades more shares per day than any other US market.[28] These companies include leaders in their respective industries such as technology, retail, financial services, transportation media and biotechnology.

According to NASDAQ Facts:[29]

- As of 30 November 2007, NASDAQ has been the market of choice for 142 initial price offerings (IPOs), representing 65% of all IPOs listing on the US market so far in 2007. In addition, 24 international companies chose NASDAQ for their public offerings, raising more than $3.6 billion. As of 30 November 2007, NASDAQ's 142 IPOs had raised a combined $18.9 billion.
- 53% of NYSE-listed securities are trading on NASDAQ as of October 2007.
- Of the approximately 3,100 listings on NASDAQ, 314 are non-US companies from 35 countries representing all industry sectors.

In 2007, NASDAQ and Swedish exchange operator OMX agreed to combine the two companies to become what is believed to be the largest global network of exchanges and exchange customers linked by technology. The rationale for the merger was to ensure that NASDAQ was not left out of the consolidation push which had led to a global rush for exchanges to partner.

Data Providers

Thomson Reuters

Thomson Reuters is a media company created by the Thomson Corporation's recent purchase of Reuters. The new company is headquartered in New York and has 50,000 employees and more than 40,000 customers in 155 countries.

Thomson Reuters sells electronic news and data such as foreign exchange and energy data to financial services companies including investment banks, hedge funds and prime brokers. It is said to be in direct competition with Bloomberg for financial clients and industry sources claim that along with Bloomberg it has a third of the global financial data market.

Reuters was founded in 1851 when Paul Julius transmitted stock market quotes on the Calais-Dover cable, having previously used pigeons to fly stock prices between Germany and Belgium. This event marked the beginning of the Reuters news service, which as of April 2008 had about 2,400 journalists, and

28 Source: NASDAQ Fact Sheet 2008.
29 Ibid.

became the foundation for a $5 billion-a-year news and financial data empire. Thomson, on the other hand, has publishing roots dating back to 1934 when a native of Toronto, Roy Thomson, bought the Timmins Press in Northern Ontario.

Dow Jones Newswires

Dow Jones Newswires is the real-time financial news organisation owned by Dow Jones. It was founded in 1882 and as of July 2005 had more than 420,000 financial professionals in 66 countries. These subscribers include brokers, analysts, private wealth managers, financial advisers and individual investors.

The company is part of the Dow Jones news network of nearly 1,900 business and financial news staff worldwide, with access to the output of more than 3,650 reporters worldwide through a 30-year partnership between the Associated Press and the Dow Jones news network.

Dow Jones Newswires produces 10,000 items daily covering equities, fixed income, foreign exchange, energy, commodities, corporate disclosure, futures and other financial markets; updated 24 hours a day, seven days a week and coverage of more than 37,000 listed companies. Selected services are supplied in 10 languages: Dutch, English, French, German, Italian, Portuguese, Spanish, Chinese, Japanese and Russian. It also contains full content from Dow Jones publications such as the Wall Street Journal, Barron's and Barron's.com, and Smart Money.

It is an invaluable resource for private wealth managers to ensure that they keep abreast of business/financial, economic and market-moving political news.

Bloomberg L.P.

Bloomberg is a leading financial news and data company. Unconfirmed sources claim that it has a 33% share of the financial news and data market. Its main competitor is Thomson Reuters.

Bloomberg was founded in 1981 when Michael R. Bloomberg decided he wanted to create an information services, news and media company that provided business and financial professionals with the tools and data they needed on a single, all-inclusive platform.[30]

The Bloomberg service is a subscription service that sells financial data and analytic software to leverage the data's usefulness. This is accessible through a colour-coded Bloomberg keyboard that pops the desired information onto a computer screen, either owned by the subscriber or one that Bloomberg provides.[31]

Financial Times

The *Financial Times* (FT) is a British international business newspaper. In the UK,

---

30 Source: http://about.bloomberg.com/index.html
31 Carol J. Loomis, (5 April 2007), "Bloomberg's Money Machine", Fortune Magazine. Available from http://money.cnn.com/magazines/fortune/fortune_archive/2007/04/16/8404302/index.htm?postversion=2007040506

it is a daily morning newspaper published in London that has had a strong influence on the financial policies of the British government and is known as one of the UK's superior daily newspapers. The periodical is printed in 23 cities. The European edition is distributed in Continental Europe, the Middle East, Africa and Asia.

Founded in 1888 by James Sheridan and his brother, the *Financial Times* competed for many years with four other finance-oriented newspapers, finally in 1945 absorbing the last of these, the Financial News (founded in 1884). The FT has specialised in reporting business and financial news while maintaining an independent editorial outlook. In 1995, the Financial Times group launched FT.com, now one of the few UK news sites successfully operating a subscription model for content.

The *Financial Times* has a sizeable network of international reporters – about 110 of its 475 journalists are based outside the UK. The FT is usually in two sections; the first section covers national and international news, while the second section covers company and markets news.

FTfm, a weekly review of the fund management industry, is a supplement to the *Financial Times* that reports on the hedge fund industry.

Central Securities Depositories
Clearstream International SA

Clearstream, headquartered in Luxembourg, is an international settlement and custody organisation offering services covering both domestic and internationally traded bonds and equities.

More than 2,500 customers in 94 countries are connected to Clearstream's global network. The value of assets held on deposit amounted to EUR 6.9 trillion as at 31 December 2002.[32]

Clearstream has developed innovative services in investment fund processing including Vestima, an STP solution for investment fund processing. It enables fund distributors to process orders rapidly, efficiently and safely.

Clearstream's latest post-trade solution, the Central Facility for Funds, was developed to provide a central settlement system that can plug into any order routing system, including Clearstream's own product Vestima+. The platform basically offers one single set of settlement and payment instructions for all eligible funds, including hedge funds, so that as well as reducing risk, the whole settlement process will be speeded up and simplified.[33]

Euroclear Bank SA

Euroclear Bank SA/NV, a Belgian credit institution headquartered in Brussels, acts as the International Central Securities Depository of the Euroclear group. Euroclear Bank offers a single access point to securities services in more than 25 equity markets and over 30 bond markets worldwide.

---

32 Source: www.ecsda.com/portal/what_is_ecsda_/members/clearstream_international_sa/
33 Source: http://globalcustody.net/default/efm-european-fund-manager_feature/

Euroclear Bank provides a range of core and value-added services including fund transaction processing through FundSettle,[34] and securities lending and borrowing facilities.

Euroclear Bank's services cover over 210,000 international and global securities from over 30 markets: debt securities, equities and investment funds.

Whilst central securities depositories such as Euroclear and Clearstream can offer funds processing services for hedge funds through their respective platforms, it should be noted that the processing of hedge fund distributions is extremely manual. It entails a lot of risks and errors and the cost of processing hedge fund transactions still remains extremely high. Furthermore, the administrators in charge of the shareholder register or fund accounting are often in "offshore" locations where technological capacities may be more limited than in traditional locations such as Europe and the USA.

Security Identifier Types

Security identifier[35] types are the various methods by which a security product or issue is identified. They are each managed and distributed by different organisations. Each country has a National Numbering Agency (NNA), which is the organisation responsible for the assignment of security identifiers to corporate security issues within its national jurisdiction. In some emerging markets, where no recognised NNA exists, a substitute agency has authority to issue numbers. Usually, central securities depositories, stock exchanges or financial publishing companies will be responsible for the maintenance of security codes. The following table illustrates the countries with their most commonly used national numbering scheme.

Country	Identifier	Character Type	Number of characters
UK	SEDOL	Numeric	7
USA	CUSIP	Alphanumeric	9
Japan	Quick Code	Numeric	5
Germany	WKN	Numeric	6
France	Euroclear France	Numeric	6
Switzerland	Valor	Numeric	9

34 FundSettle is a fully integrated platform for the straight-through processing of fund transactions.

35 The security identifiers discussed above should not be confused with a Security Identifier (commonly abbreviated to SID), which is a unique name (an alphanumeric character string) that is assigned by a Windows Domain controller during the log-on process and used to identify an object, such as a user or a group of users in a network of NT/2008 systems.

CUSIP

The acronym CUSIP stands for Committee on Uniform Securities Identification Procedures and the 9-character alphanumeric security identifiers that they distribute for all North American securities for the purposes of facilitating clearing and settlement of trades. The CUSIP distribution system is owned by the American Bankers' Association and is operated by Standard & Poor's. The CUSIP Services Bureau acts as the NNA for North America, and the CUSIP serves as the National Securities Identification Number for products issued from both the United States and Canada.

The CUSIP number acts as a sort of DNA for the security – uniquely identifying the company or issuer and the type of security. The first six characters are known as the "base" (or "CUSIP-6"), and uniquely identify the issuer. Issuer codes are assigned alphabetically from a series that includes deliberate built-in "gaps" for future expansion. The last two characters of the issuer code can be letters, in order to provide more room for expansion. The numbers from 990000 up are reserved, as are xxx990 and up within each group of 1000 (i.e. 100990 to 1009ZZ).

An example of a CUSIP number is 594918104, which is allocated to Microsoft.

ISIN

ISO 6166, the ISO standard that the International Organisation for Standardisation required to bring uniform structure to international securities identification while preserving the sovereignty of local numbering agencies to manage assets within their markets, created the rules for the International Securities Number (ISIN). The ISIN is the all-encompassing standard that combines the code assigned by a local National Numbering Agency with the ISO country code of the security issuer's domicile. A check digit is added to the standard to ensure data integrity.

An example of an ISIN number is US4592001014 derived thus:

/Country code of issuer: US/ + /CUSIP: 459200101/+/check digit calculated from algorithm: 4/

SEDOL

SEDOL, which stands for Stock Exchange Daily Official List, is an identification code, consisting of seven alphanumeric characters, that is assigned to all securities trading on the London Stock Exchange and on other smaller exchanges in the UK. The numbers are assigned by the London Stock Exchange, on request by the security issuer. SEDOLs serve as the National Securities Identifying Number (NSIN) for all securities issued in the United Kingdom and are therefore part of the security's ISIN as well.

ISINs were to be used to replace SEDOL. However, since a single ISIN is used to identify the shares of a company regardless of the exchange it is being traded on, it was impossible to specify a trade on a particular exchange or currency. This was identified as a problem and this, amongst other issues, forced a reversal of this decision. A solution to this problem is being sought by way of expansion of the ISIN standard.

SEDOL is also used to identify foreign stocks, especially those that aren't actively traded in the USA and don't have a CUSIP number.

RIC

RIC stands for Reuters Instrument Code, a ticker-like code used by Reuters to identify financial instruments and indices. The RIC is made up primarily of the security's ticker symbol, optionally followed by a period and exchange code based on the name of the stock exchange which uses that ticker. For instance, DGE.N is a valid RIC, referring to DIAGEO being traded on the New York Stock Exchange. DGE.L refers to the same stock trading on the London Stock Exchange.

Trends in Prime Brokerage

This chapter discusses some of the recent trends in the prime brokerage industry.

Introduction

Prime brokerage has become one of the most fiercely competitive sectors in investment banking. The movement of hedge funds into the mainstream is partly responsible for this trend. The value of assets under management by European hedge funds, for instance, was estimated to be $450 billion by the end of 2007 and they may have contributed 15–20% of investment banking revenue in the same year. Prime brokerage revenues for 2007, as a consequence, were estimated to have been about $8.5 billion.[25] As seen in previous chapters, prime brokerage divisions are also their banks' main route to selling other services to hedge funds as the latter have gone from being niche investors to becoming among the most important clients.

To sustain these levels of revenue and increase their offerings to hedge funds, prime brokerage divisions of investment banks have to be aware of the recent trends that have been shaping the prime brokerage industry.

A discussion follows of a number of these trends.

The Rising Importance of Prime Brokerage as a Banking Business Line

by Ann C. Logue

Investment banks are as fond of hedge funds as pension funds are, but for very different reasons. Where an institutional investor sees the potential for return, a bank sees a nice healthy stream of low-risk fees for prime brokerage services rendered. As stated elsewhere, prime brokerage involves securities lending and trade settlement for institutional investors including hedge funds, and it's one of the fastest-growing segments for most full-service investment banks. Let's face it: the value of equity research has declined, the mortgage securities business has collapsed, and the deal-making business is subject to economic whims. Prime brokerage will grow as long as hedge funds collect assets.

In addition to generating fees, prime brokerage complements existing business lines and that gives the largest of the large investment banks an ongoing competitive advantage. Although not all prime brokerage customers are hedge funds (many money management firms use prime brokerage services), the hedge funds generate more fees per account because the managers tend to trade more frequently. Because hedge funds are the fastest-growing money management segment, the managers are getting more dollars to trade.

Hedge fund investors care about the choice of prime broker, too. They want to know that the fund taking their money has systems in place to handle assets

36 Source: City and Financial.

appropriately and account for trades. In some of the bigger frauds, it turned out that the hedge fund didn't use an established prime broker, which should have been a warning. For example, in February 2006 the Securities and Exchange Commission charged a hedge fund, International Management Associates, and its manager, Kirk Wright, with fraud. One indication of trouble was that instead of using a prime broker, the fund's accounts were kept at E*Trade, AmeriTrade and other brokerage firms that specialise in services for individual investors, not investment companies.

Prime Brokerage by the Numbers

Prime brokerage is big business. In 2007, Morgan Stanley reported that total sales and trading revenues were up 38% to $8.7 billion, driven in large part by the prime brokerage business. This is just a fraction of the firm's $28.0 billion in revenues, but it is growing faster than the firm as a whole. In 2006, Morgan Stanley's sales and trading revenues were up 31% to $6.3 billion out of total revenues of $29.8 billion. The firm credited prime brokerage for driving growth that year, too.

Merrill Lynch had similar results. The firm's total 2007 revenues were considerably lower than those reported in 2006 because of write-downs in various collateralised debt obligation assets. Prime brokerage thrived amidst the chaos: in 2007, Merrill's equity market revenues, which included prime brokerage, were up 45% to $8.3 billion, up 23% from the $6.7 billion posted in 2006.

Interested in building scale, JPMorgan Chase saw that prime brokerage was one of the key assets to be gained in the Bear Stearns bailout. Bear Stearns' global equities division, which included prime brokerage, generated $3.36 billion in revenue in 2007. JPMorgan Chase accounts for prime brokerage in its treasury and securities division, which had 2007 revenues of $6.9 billion.

Prime brokerage is big business on its face, and it steers revenue elsewhere in the firm. It's more difficult to quantify the ancillary effects of a stronger wealth management business because of capital introduction services or more sales and trading volume because of the business relationship, but they can't be dismissed.

Prime Brokerage offers Fat, Stable Margins

Investment banks report their prime brokerage revenues, but not the profits. They have to be good for banks that have a large-enough business to benefit from scale economies, or they wouldn't be trying to increase their prime brokerage accounts. Prime brokerage revenues are driven by fees for service and have good economies of scale. (One reason that small brokerage firms, financial planners, and money management firms have long had outside clearing or prime broker arrangements is that they can't generate enough volume on their own to cover the costs.) The prime broker takes relatively little risk; it mostly processes paperwork and lends securities for very short periods of time. It's nicely predictable as long as hedge funds have assets that need to be invested, too.

The main source of fees for most prime brokers comes from interest on the margin loans that hedge funds take in order to buy more securities. Most hedge funds use leverage as a matter of course. Of course, the prime broker has to have the cash to lend, favouring firms that have significant assets and lines of credit to draw on. The more prime brokerage that a bank has, the more experience it has with exotic securities and complex trading strategies. That helps the bank manage risk better; it also attracts hedge funds that need confidence that their more creative ideas will be executed and accounted for appropriately.

For fund managers who want to sell short, the prime broker will happily lend them the securities that they need to do it, charging interest all the while. Hedge funds usually trade with several different brokerage firms (the better to collect more information about what's happening in the markets), but it's too unwieldy to manage all of the accounts everywhere. A prime broker will settle trades no matter where they are made, levying a fee for that service, too. Finally, the prime broker will prepare account records and related paperwork that the hedge fund needs to calculate performance and create reports for its investors. And yes, that comes at a price.

Prime brokerage margins are so attractive that some prime brokers even provide office space, software and other services to help a nascent hedge fund get going in the hope that it becomes a big future customer. These services don't provide extra revenues, but they may help keep the fees for traditional prime brokerage services from falling into commodity-pricing territory. Start-up services help the new fund harness more resources to get larger faster while helping the broker take a tighter hold on the customer.

Feeding Customers to Business Units

Investment banks are in the business of making money, and prime brokerage isn't the only way a bank makes money from hedge funds. Prime brokerage customers use sales and trading services and participate in underwritings, other key business units for investment banks. And, the investment bank may have wealth management customers interested in placing money with those hedge funds.

No matter who its prime broker is, a hedge fund is going to do business with other investment banks. But on the margin, it might be more likely to take a call from the firm that clears its trades and processes its paperwork than from the firm's competitor. Investment banks have many products to sell (which is why they are collectively known as "the sell side"). If a firm's underwriting department is trying to get a deal done, or if the trading desk has a block of stock to sell, those relationships with hedge funds might pay off.

One way that many prime brokers attract hedge funds as customers is through their capital introduction services, which let hedge fund managers meet the firm's high-net-worth individual and institutional clients at conferences and seminars. It's great for a fund that's struggling to collect assets, but it also helps the bank. The more investment options it can offer to wealth management clients, the more reasons that folks with big assets have to work with the bank.

Competition and Consolidation

Making matches between investors and funds is a nice selling proposition, but that's not where the big profits sit. Prime brokerage flourishes when economies of scale are in place. Those that can grow the business will show accelerating profits as they push more fee-generating transactions through their high fixed-cost information systems. That's why the largest prime brokers are likely to expand while the smaller ones sell out or shut down. For example, ABN Amro sold its prime brokerage business to UBS in 2006, and JPMorgan Chase eyed Bear Stearns' prime brokerage business when it agreed to take over the ailing firm. As troubled institutions shed businesses and stronger ones merge, there will be fewer and larger prime brokers.

Consolidation won't lead to one or two brokers with all of the business, though. Because prime brokers are also trading for their own accounts and dealing with other customers, information about any one hedge fund's activities can become valuable currency. That's good for the broker and bad for the hedge funds. Hence, many hedge funds are choosing to deal with several prime brokers, the better to divide up trading activity so that no one broker knows exactly what the fund is doing. That may also help the hedge funds negotiate for lower fees.

Increasing Demand for Prime Brokerage Services in Credit Derivatives Market

Hedge funds have been one of the drivers for growth in the credit derivatives market. Investment banks have been keen to exploit this trend by providing credit derivatives prime brokerage platforms to help minimise the burden for hedge funds of confirming, processing and settling trades with multiple counterparties.

What are Credit Derivatives?

Industry experts believe that the development of credit derivatives is a logical extension of the ever-growing range of derivatives in the financial market. Derivatives produce a completely independent trade in the risks/return of an asset. An example is that a trade in options in equities may run completely independently of trades in equity shares.

Credit derivatives apply the same concept to a credit asset. A credit asset is the asset that a credit provider creates. Examples of credit assets include loans given by banks and bonds held by capital markets participants. A credit derivative allows for elimination of the risk of default (and additional risks, depending on the type of derivative) from the loan or the bond in a way that the risk gets transferred to the counterparty and the loan or the bond continues to be held by the holder or originator of these assets. In a credit transaction, the counterparty buys the risk for a premium, this premium representing the rewards of the counterparty. Therefore, credit derivatives are essentially vehicles for transferring risks and rewards in credit assets, namely loans or bonds, to other financial market participants.

There are different definitions of credit derivatives, but the one that appears to be the most accurate is as follows:

Credit derivatives is a general term used to describe various swap and option contracts designed to transfer credit risk on loans or other assets from one party, the protection buyer, to another party, the protection seller. The protection seller receives a premium or interest-related payments in return for contracting to make payments to the protection buyer, which are linked to the credit standing of a reference asset or assets. (The Financial Services Authority)

The following is a brief description of the various types of credit derivative:

- **Credit default swap:** This is a swap designed to transfer the credit exposure of fixed income products between parties. It involves two parties entering into an agreement whereby one party pays the other a fixed periodic coupon for the specified life of the agreement. The other party makes no payments unless a specified credit event occurs. Credit events are typically defined to include a material default, bankruptcy or debt restructuring for a specified reference asset. If such a credit event occurs, the party makes a payment to the first party, and the swap then terminates.
- **Credit-linked note:** This is a debt instrument that is bundled with an embedded credit derivative, allowing the issuer to transfer a specific credit risk to credit investors. It can be described as a type of funded credit derivative in which the investor in the note, the credit protection seller, makes an upfront payment to the issuer of the note, the protection buyer. If no credit event occurs during the life of the note, the redemption value of the note is paid to the investor upon maturity.
- **Total return swap (TRS):** This is a bilateral agreement where one party (the TRS payer) agrees to pay the other (the TRS receiver) the total return of a defined asset in return for receiving a stream of, for example, LIBOR-based cash flows. It is a mechanism for the TRS receiver to enjoy the economic benefits of owning an asset without utilising the balance sheet. The TRS receiver is seeking returns on the asset without buying the asset.

Global Market Growth

According to the British Bankers' Association, at the end of 2008 the global credit derivatives market will have expanded to $33 trillion. It expects this growth to continue beyond this year. In addition, it expects the diversity of the products to continue to grow.

The expansion of index trades, tranched index trades and equity-linked products – to highlight but a few – has created an unprecedented variety of traded products in the credit derivatives market.

Hedge funds have become a major force in the credit derivatives market and their share of the volume in both buying and selling credit protection increased by almost 100% between 2004 and 2006, according to the BBA Credit Derivatives Report 2006.

With regard to the product range as of 2006, single-name credit default swaps represented a substantial section of the global credit derivatives market. Index trades also became the second largest product, representing 30% of the

first quarter of 2006 (see Table 6.1). Figure 6.2 also shows the market share of the product range at the end of 2006 and forecasts for the end of 2008.

Figure 6.1 Global Credit Derivatives Market from 1996 to 2008

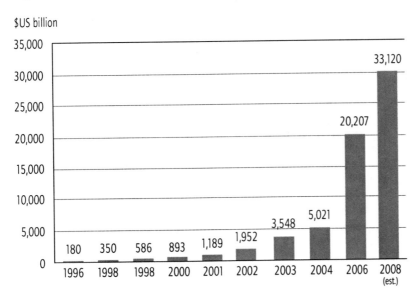

Source: British Bankers' Association

Table 6.1

Type	2000	2002	2004	2006
Basket products	6.0%	6.0%	4.0%	1.8%
Credit linked notes	10.0%	8.0%	6.0%	3.1%
Credit spread options	5.0%	5.0%	2.0%	1.3%
Equity linked credit products	n/a	n/a	1.0%	0.4%
Full index trades	n/a	n/a	9.0%	30.1%
Single-name credit default swaps	38.0%	45.0%	51.0%	32.9%
Swaptions	n/a	n/a	1.0%	0.8%
Synthetic CDOs – full capital	n/a	n/a	6.0%	3.7%
Synthetic CDOs –partial capital	n/a	n/a	10.0%	12.6%
Tranched index trades	n/a	n/a	2.0%	7.6%
Others	41.0%	36.0%	8.0%	5.7%

Source: British Bankers' Association

Hedge funds have found that staying on top of trade confirmations in a fast-growing market is a difficult challenge and levels of unsigned confirmations in the credit confirmations could become burdensome. However the burden is not

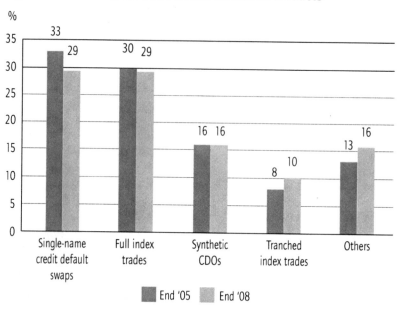

Figure 6.2 Market Shares of Credit Derivatives Products

Source: British Bankers' Association

just administrative. Supposing a hedge fund puts on trades with multiple counterparties; it needs to confirm and settle each trade individually as well as post collateral and margin with each dealer. The counterparties are not capable of taking into account offsetting trades between various dealers, resulting in an uneconomical use of the fund's capital.

The increasing demand for prime brokerage services in the credit derivatives markets is underscored by the need to margin those trades that may involve one counterparty with whom the hedge fund is long and another with whom it is short as stand-alone transactions, despite being low-risk trades and the fact that the two counterparties cannot see the other components of the trade.

This is one of the major reasons for the increased demand for prime brokerage services in the credit derivatives market. Prime brokerage divisions of investment banks have been reacting to the increased demand by creating platforms that take over the bulk of the back-office burden for hedge fund managers. An essential aspect is the enabling of a broker to step in and act as counterparty for all the hedge fund's trades. The investment bank can then compute the margin, factoring in all the trades in the hedge fund's portfolio. Analysis from a portfolio perspective would reveal that any offsetting trades would result in lower margin payments.

It is worth noting that the style of prime brokerage offering and the extent can differ significantly. While some prime brokers offer a full intermediation[37] service for derivatives, enabling them to act as counterparty for any of the hedge fund's trades in addition to transaction processing and reporting services, others offer similar functionality with the investment bank acting as financing and settlement agent, settling trades on behalf of the hedge fund. Depending whether there are leveraging requirements or not, the prime broker can also provide financing. This, in effect, provides opportunities for the hedge fund to outsource much of its back office and the prime broker can then take responsibility.

In the absence of a prime brokerage facility, the hedge fund would usually receive documentation from the executing broker that provides a description of the transition – for example describing the cashflows and naming the underlying reference obligation and so on. Confirmation and agreement of the terms are the next steps and thereafter the documentation is sent back and the trade completed.

The impact of an efficient prime brokerage platform is profound if the hedge fund is trading across a variety of structured credit markets. The hedge fund allows the prime broker to intermediate in not just single-name credit default swaps but also index tranching products and credit options.

Despite the back-office problems experienced by the credit derivatives market in recent times, industry observers believe that initiatives such as the Depository Trust and Clearing Corporation (DTCC) deriv/SERV matching service and the ISDA's novation protocol will bring about radical changes in the industry.

ISDA's novation protocol is designed to standardise the passing of rights and obligations to a third party. If a hedge fund wishes to exit a CDS deal before maturity, it can transfer the contract to another entity rather than terminate it.[38] In the past, these kinds of transfer would need the written approval of the three parties involved in the deal before the fund could assign the trade. The novation protocol allows for an electronic communication between parties involved, hence simplifying the requirements.

The Rise of FX Prime Brokerage

FX prime brokerage is an important aspect of foreign exchange trading. As the FX markets have become more explosive, investment banks have been beefing up increasingly competitive prime brokerage services for foreign exchange as they strive to win lucrative hedge fund clients that trade FX, and boost flows to sustain their position as big market players.

The highly liquid foreign exchange market has in recent times been the target for banks reinforcing their prime brokerage services, in which they offer their hedge fund clients access and administration services in return for fees. In addition, the higher volatility in recent years has made currencies an asset class in

---

37 This is when a prime broker allows the hedge fund to use its balance sheet and credit rating when it approaches a trading counterparty.

38 Source: Prime Brokerage (February 2006), Risk.

their own right as opposed to simply a vehicle for investing in overseas markets.

FX prime brokerage has grown rapidly since its inception in the early 1990s. Initially, it was a low-key, informal arrangement between individual institutions, but has since evolved into a booming business for investment banks. One of the major drivers for the rise of prime brokerage was the sharp fall in stocks in the early part of the decade and the low returns in bonds from low interest rates worldwide, which prompted investors to focus on volatile and liquid currencies as profit generators. Hence, currency management has a greater emphasis on adding value, having evolved from a risk reduction exercise. Investors have now accepted currency as an asset class that can provide added value and one that is not correlated with equities and bonds. Currencies are a relatively new asset class, unlike established asset classes such as bonds and stocks. Major currencies only floated free at the end of the 1944 Bretton Woods[39] system in 1971.

According to industry sources, in 1997 fewer than 10 organisations in the global marketplace used a foreign exchange prime broker, and the market was dominated by 4 banks. However, by 2005 it was estimated that between 250 and 600 clients used prime brokerage services and at least 20 different banks were providing the services as a core foreign-exchange product.[40]

FX prime brokerage can be described as an arrangement under which foreign exchange deals of a hedge fund are transacted with a single bank counterparty (the prime broker), even though they may initially be agreed between the hedge fund and a third-party bank. It allows the hedge fund to initiate trades, subject to credit limits, with a group of third-party banks in the prime broker's name.[41]

A diagrammatic representation of the process is shown in Figure 6.3.

Figure 6.3 FX Prime Brokerage Process

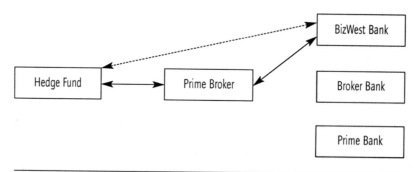

---

39 The Bretton Woods system of monetary management established the rules for commercial and financial relations among the world's major industrial states. The Bretton Woods system was the first example of a fully negotiated monetary order intended to govern monetary relations among independent nation-states.
40 Source: Foreign Exchange Joint Standing Committee e-commerce subgroup report.
41 Ibid.

The process is described thus:

1. The hedge fund initially agrees a transaction with a third-party bank, in the name of the prime broker.
2. The transaction is then logged by the prime broker.
3. In the final phase of the process, a reciprocal transaction is entered into between the hedge fund and the prime broker.

This process has advantages from an administration point of view of the hedge fund, in that legally its transactions are executed with a single counterparty, i.e. the prime broker. The hedge fund's net position maybe rolled forward by using FX swaps, pending the time the hedge fund reverses its original trade; or settlement may be effected at regular intervals, for example at the end of the month. Collateralisation may be involved. However, prime brokerage also gives the hedge fund, which can have a low credit rating, the opportunity to initiate trades with a wider range of counterparties, because it is in effect assuming (borrowing) the credit rating of the prime broker bank. This implies, among other things, that it is confident of dealing at an attractive rate. The prime broker process delineates the provision of liquidity (in Figure 6.3 provided by Bizwest bank) from the provision of credit by the prime broker.

FX brokerage is discussed further in Chapter 7.

Use of FX Prime Brokerage to Implement Currency Overlay

Despite the increasing popularity of foreign exchange prime brokerage in the absolute return universe, the currency overlay industry appears to be oblivious to this trend. Industry experts are baffled with this attitude to the trend.

What is Currency Overlay?

Currency overlay is the management of currency risk that already exists in an international portfolio.

This involves managing the currency exposures separately from the underlying assets. The risk inherent in the portfolio stems from the fact that portfolio managers like hedge funds seek diversification from their assets. For instance, a UK pound sterling-based hedge fund may decide to overweight its exposure to US equities. This decision is based primarily on the prospects for the US equity without factoring in the effect of currency fluctuation. In terms of currency exposure that needs to be managed, suppose that the US equity exposure appreciated by 20% from a local currency perspective (US dollar) during, say, the holiday period. However if, during the sale period, the US dollar has depreciated by 20% against the UK pound sterling, then it can be concluded that the return generated from the US dollar that is positive will be completely offset by the depreciation that resulted in a loss.

Traditionally, investors have failed to recognise the underlying currency risk in their international portfolios in the hope that currency effects will even out over time. This might be the case, but over a significant number of years that could be a longer time period than most investors' investment horizons. There could be large fluctuations during this time with which investors may not be comfortable. This presents opportunities for skilled currency overlay managers. The main reason for pursuing a currency overlay strategy is to limit currency losses and maximise currency gain.

FX prime brokerage reduces the settlement risk for hedge funds that implement currency overlay and maintain credit lines for foreign exchange trading at more than one financial institution. When the overlay manager liquidates a client position, which was initiated with a different bank, the client is responsible for the delivery and settlement of currency balances on value day for both contracts.

The following diagrams depict the transaction flow before the use of FX prime brokerage in a currency overlay program and after the use of FX prime brokerage.

Figure 6.4 Transaction Flow before Prime Brokerage

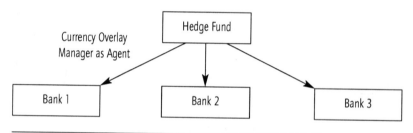

Figure 6.5 Transaction Flow after Prime Brokerage

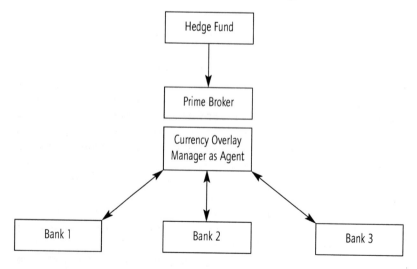

A typical example is if a currency overlay manager undertakes a GBP-USD transaction on behalf of a client such as a hedge fund, buys 10 million GBP from one bank and later closes that position by selling GBP with a different bank; the responsibility of the GBP and USD payments lies with the clients. The responsibility and the associated risk are removed by dealing through a prime brokerage relationship. The appointed banks under the prime brokerage facility will now only recognise transactions with the prime broker. The client is without any obligation in the event of one bank making an error in delivery or failing completely. The client's only risk is for the net position with the prime broker, given that all trades are in and out with the clearer. In this example, the only exposure would be the net USD amount from the two trades. (The GBP balances net to zero.)

Prime Brokers Servicing Traditional Asset Managers

One recent trend that is radically shaking up the prime brokerage business is the desire of prime brokers to service traditional asset managers, in addition to their hedge fund clients. The emphasis will be on the former's derivative activity.

Industry watchers agree that the inability of custodian banks and fund administrators to meet the buy-side clients' increasing demand for derivatives processing could create huge opportunities for prime brokers. Given that prime brokers are already involved in buy-side servicing when attached to hedge funds, they are positioned to meet the challenge of servicing traditional asset managers.

One aspect of fulfilling the derivatives processing needs of asset managers that could be a stumbling block is the low margins, given that the use of derivatives by traditional asset managers follows a different template to hedge funds. Prime brokers may not find the revenue streams for this job attractive when they compare it to the revenues derived from the trading style of hedge funds, which is closer to the investment banking model. Investment banks view the prime brokerage business as high volume/high margin and do not consider asset derivatives administration to be in this category.

Another thorny issue is the capital outlays required to perform the back-office administration functions for higher volume asset managers, despite the platforms that prime brokerage currently have in place to manage transactions.

Industry experts question the possibility of prime brokers becoming one-stop shops for traditional asset managers in the same way as they are for hedge funds. The argument is based on the need for prime brokers to assess the cost of creating different accounting and administrative platforms in various regions in order to fulfil the multi-jurisdictional requirements of large asset managers, plus their relatively higher number of funds.

Furthermore, the issue of pricing could potentially be another obstacle in their quest for widening their client base to include traditional asset managers. Prime brokers are aware of the challenges in the pricing structure they need to adopt for their services to asset managers, since this will determine the attractiveness or viability of prime brokerage as a solution for asset managers. They need to perform a thorough review of the current levels of fees they charge.

In times of market volatility, there is the need for confidence in valuations and in the administration of derivatives positions as they are major components of a thriving market. This is where prime brokers that are part of a financial services firm that also has a custodial arm can have a competitive edge provided their cost structures are attractive, especially for derivatives valuations. While the servicing and valuations of many vanilla swaps and derivatives is reasonably uncomplicated and generally available, it is the complex derivatives trades that some asset managers use that merit some careful considerations when determining the pricing of the positions, as it should reflect the increased complexity and risk.

Capacity, however, is not an issue as most prime brokers have the extra capacity to cope with the asset management business; they just need to segregate the various departments.

The Emergence of 130/30 Strategies

Some experts attribute the increase in demand for prime brokerage services to an explosion in trading volumes as well as the increase in the number of traditional fund managers venturing into the hedge fund space. These traditional fund managers are looking to compete against hedge funds by creating long/short products.

An interesting aspect of this trend is that while conventional managers are entering the hedge fund marketplace, hedge funds are also going back into the conventional long-only space, creating new opportunities for prime brokers. Increasingly prime brokers are marketing not only to hedge funds, but also to private equity and long-only firms as well.

The emergence of 130/30 strategies is allowing hedge funds to attract more funds from institutional investors, and larger traditional fund managers are also seeing these products as a way of getting into the hedge fund space. Thus, the appearance of 130/30 strategies on the investment landscape is confirmation of the blurring of the lines between traditional and alternative strategies. It contests the role of traditional managers who stick to the old rules and focus on outperforming benchmarks via sector and security selection.

What is 130/30?

A 130/30 strategy has now become a universal accepted term for conventional long-only strategies that are at liberty to permit short selling. The strategy can be defined as follows:

A strategy that uses financial leverage by shorting poor performing stocks and purchasing shares that are expected to have high returns. A 130/30 ratio implies shorting stocks up to 30% of the portfolio value and then using the funds to take a long position in the stocks the investor feels will outperform the market. (Investopedia.com)

It should be noted that while 130/30 specifies a mandate in which 130% of the value of a portfolio is held in long positions and 30% in short positions, there are many other solutions. Similar portfolios usually range from 120/20 to 140/40 and they follow the same convention of holding long and short positions. Nevertheless, no matter what the degree of shorting is, these strategies typically maintain a 100% net market exposure which means that the amount shorted is matched by an increment of equal value on the long side.

Figure 6.6 Mechanics of a 130/30 portfolio

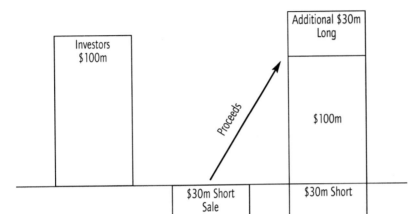

- 100% net market exposure
- $60m additional active bets
- Beta = 1.0

Source: Evaluation Associates LLC

Opportunities for Prime Brokers

The increasing popularity of 130/30 translates into increased volumes of business for prime brokers. It provides an opportunity for them to service traditional funds that never needed prime brokerage services. They also get to educate the traditional fund managers on the services that prime brokerage can offer and at the same time speak to these fund managers about creating 130/30 funds.

Investing in 130/30 strategies entails extra operational requirements and complexities, many of which are in the realms of prime brokerage. In addition, a traditional custodian cannot hold short positions; thus any strategy that involves short selling requires a prime broker. The establishment of an effective relationship between a prime broker and an investor, traditional or hedge fund manager, utilising a 130/30 strategy involves:

- confidence in the prime broker's ability to source the securities the fund manager intends to short;
- the borrowing costs and the fee structure in general;
- the availability and quality of the services provided.

There are, without question, opportunities in the market for unconstrained strategies such as 130/30 for prime brokers to exploit. Estimates of assets in unconstrained strategies range from £15 billion to £25 billion.

The Advent of the Multi-Prime Brokerage Environment

In the past, it was conventional practice for a hedge fund to make use of more than one executing broker and a single prime broker. Nowadays, a number of hedge funds have discovered the merits of working with multiple prime brokers, as well. By spreading its servicing requirements among multiple prime brokers, a hedge fund can successfully leverage its access to the valuable resources from multiple providers.

One of the major drivers for hedge funds adopting a multi-prime broker environment is that hedge fund managers continue to pursue opportunities by

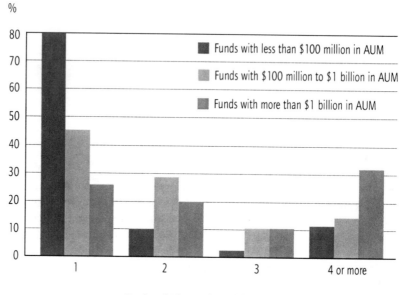

Figure 6.7 Number of Prime Broker Relationships by Fund Size

Source: Greenwich Associates study commissioned on behalf of Merrill Lynch, 2006

expanding into strategies that promise higher returns and at the same time manage their operating costs in a fast-changing and demanding business environment. At the core of any hedge fund's operations is its reliance on the prime broker and in the case of larger funds, reliance on multiple prime brokers. As for smaller hedge funds, the structural challenges of engaging a second or third prime broker can be exorbitant and the preference for the comfort of staying in an existing relationship is seen an advantage. Size will no longer be the determinant for utilising multiple prime brokers, but in the face of increased industry and investor demand, all hedge funds will, and are inclined to have, at least two or three or even more prime brokers to meet their servicing requirements.

Making the transition to a multi-prime broker operational environment is not without its attendant challenges; a notable one being the requirement to aggregate position, cash balance and risk data into consolidated reports. Nevertheless, industry experts agree that such challenges can be overcome. Many opine that the process of adopting a multi-prime strategy can usually be a vehicle for reducing the reliance on external service providers, providing the fund with greater control over its operations. This is crucial to the expansion of the fund, particularly as there is an increasing global trend of institutional investors demanding a "best practice" back- and middle-office environment prior to investing.

A study commissioned by Greenwich Associates on behalf of Merrill Lynch in 2006 indicated that 75% of hedge funds with more that $1 billion in assets under management engage at least two prime brokers and more than 35% of those funds use four or more. A number of the smaller funds included in the survey also utilised multiple prime brokers. See Figure 6.7.

Factors Responsible for the Trend towards using Multiple Prime Brokers

At inception, hedge funds usually patronise a single prime broker. This type of relationship can be described as symbiotic given that the hedge fund receives a significant level of services that breed loyalty and, in turn, the prime broker acquires the fund's entire asset balances. The initial prime broker gets a great degree of loyalty from this relationship given that the new fund's operating procedures develop around the trading, risk and reporting tools offered by the prime broker. Despite the close relationship, most hedge funds, as they grow in size, discover that the strategic benefits of working with more than a single prime broker outweigh the expenditure involved in making operational changes.

Hedge fund managers that are looking to effectively compete, and grow their business to become more institutionalised, expand their interest into diverse strategies, markets and instruments.

For this they require the most competitive prime brokerage services (such as rates, technology, stock availability for shorting etc.), adding second and third prime brokers to fulfil their needs. Additionally, in order to obtain the best services, fund managers believe they must diversify the exposure of their portfolio by spreading across multiple prime brokers.

Hedge funds that are heavily involved in the securities lending business find that utilising multiple prime brokers gives them access to additional sources of borrowing and better pricing, as individual prime brokerage firms have different inventories of lendable securities, with some inventories deeper than others. While some specialise in hard-to-borrow securities, others may specialise in non-equity securities. In addition, engaging additional prime brokers promotes a desire to proactively search for dividend enhancement opportunities.

Hedge funds are able to assert pricing pressures on the initial prime broker that signed up at inception by introducing additional prime brokers. This aids the fund in achieving optimal financing through competitive pricing as sole mandates with a prime broker, especially a top-tier prime broker, would involve paying a premium for their services.

Furthermore, the types of services and their relative strength differ across prime brokers. Firms have differing capabilities regarding synthetic financing, swap trading, local market access or direct market access (DMA) trading tools. The way in which offsetting positions can reduce collateral requirements and cross-margin policies may also differ among prime brokers. Plus, hedge funds can make the most of capital utilisation by allowing whichever prime broker provides the best margin or collateral relief for any particular position to hold custody of a group of securities.

From a risk standpoint, the use of multiple prime brokers provides the benefits of mitigating several types of risk. Having financial relationships with multiple prime brokers helps to minimise funding liquidity risk and could also be vital should there be any distress in the markets. Operationally, using multiple prime brokers can help reconcile corporate action processing, ensuring minimal omission of any corporate action. Also, if reliance on a single prime is avoided, a hedge fund has the option of calling upon another in the event of a business interruption, exemplified by the 9/11 events of 2001. Finally, spreading fund balances across multiple prime brokers guarantees that no single investment bank has a complete view of a hedge fund's entire portfolio, an advantage from the point of view of the fund manager's reassurance when working with a prime broker that also carries out proprietary trading.

Challenges and Issues

Industry experts maintain that despite the fact that a price point cannot be attached to engaging a second or third prime broker; there are additional expenses in the form of people, processes, and systems. Usually, an additional prime broker results in:

- additional documents/counterparty monitoring;
- increased error rate in the back office;
- increased complications with regard to trade booking and allocation;
- challenges associated with portfolio aggregation and reporting;
- an increased number of contacts and interfaces with the additional prime broker(s);

■ increased pressure on staff and systems from reconciliation with multiple prime brokers.

Hedge funds find that they do not get any help from brokers in surmounting the above challenges. Therefore, most hedge funds feel it is prudent to defer the addition of a second prime broker until it is feasible for their business operation. However, in an industry that is characterised by a fast pace and constant change, thriving fund managers need to be in a position to react, despite the challenges they might face in adding extra prime brokers.

Figure 6.8 The Complexity of using Multiple Prime Brokers (2006)

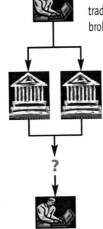

Using a single prime broker

Hedge fund manager directs all trades to a single prime broker.

Prime broker has all of the fund assets on its platform and can provide a full suite of tools (encompasses all of the fund assets), including trading, real-time P/L, collateral management, risk, and performance attribution, to the fund manager

Using multiple prime brokers

Hedge fund manager directs trades to multiple prime brokers.

Because the assets are split among multiple prime brokers, the fund manager now needs to acquire technology to aggregate the data and achieve the same level of service and transparency as the manager had in a single-prime environment.

Source: Tower Group

Industry observers believe the proliferation of the much-trumpeted open architecture platform, which is supposed to be designed to support hedge funds' requirements for multiple prime brokers, has failed to materialise.

Continued Evolution of Securities Lending Market

Securities lending provides liquidity to the equity, bond and money markets, which means it is positioned at the core of today's financial systems. This increased liquidity results in a reduction of the cost of trading, and in so doing increases market efficiency. Securities lending also provides the ability for investors to express negative views as well as positive ones. The securities lending industry is a huge, over-the-counter and well-regulated market with over €14 trillion of lendable assets available, with an average of €3 trillion assets on loan on a daily basis.[42]

The rationale behind the creation of the securities lending market was initially based on providing the means for securities lending houses to avert settlement failure, but in recent times the largest demand for borrowing now comes from planned trading strategies. The securities lending business supports a number of these types of strategies by lending shares to provide cover for transactions whereby the seller is not in possession of the shares. It is usual practice for a broker/dealer to identify demand and intermediate in the facilitation of loans for end-users like hedge funds. It is also not uncommon for prime brokers to regularly borrow securities to hedge exposure that originates from the creation of derivative instruments. This type of borrowing demand is typically fulfilled via lending agents, whose role is aggregation of lendable securities from asset owners and negotiation of prices on behalf of lending agents. Custodian banks and investment managers can act as lending agents.

One of the major trends that is responsible for the continued evolution of securities lending in the global marketplace is the margin and arbitrage opportunities in emerging Asian markets. There appears to be significant potential in Asian markets, given the widening of spreads and the increase in demand for local securities. In addition, the recent increase in the level of global investing in Asia and the increase in volume of assets made available for lending make the continent a fertile ground for players looking to get involved in securities lending. In response, regulators in the region have embraced securities lending as a critical element in increasing liquidity and an effective vehicle to encourage international investment.

Industry experts assert that Asian markets are at different stages of developing their regulatory structures and market practices. In recent times, Korea and Taiwan have altered their legal, securities and tax regulations to accommodate securities lending. Other countries in the region are reported to be seeking to follow suit. Regulators in this region that emulate the Taiwanese and Korean model will notice a faster time-to-market. In addition, a model that includes the requirements of foreign lenders and borrowers will be a key reason for success.

The Hong Kong market has witnessed exponential growth in recent years. One of the reasons for this growth is that companies in China have begun listing on the Hang Seng Index.[43] There has been demand for market exposure to China in recent years and the Hang Seng provides the medium.

---

42 Dr Bill Cuthbert and Michelle Napier, Spitalfields Advisors, from "How Big is the Securities Lending Market?", presentation delivered at The Securities Lending Forum, 20 March 2007.
43 The capitalisation-weighted index in the Hong Kong stock market.

In the absence of an efficient stock lending infrastructure on a par with the mature markets of North America and Europe, short interest[44] is usually synthetically derived using swaps. A number of progressive fund managers will enter swaps on their long positions. The prime brokers can then sell the long positions on behalf of the hedge fund to generate the short position. Swaps are the most common instrument used when regular stock lending is not an acceptable practice in a particular market.

Each Asian market has its own peculiarity and dynamics. For example, automatic buy-ins[45] in Singapore and Hong Kong, T +1 settlement in Taiwan and trading through the Korea Securities Depository in Korea. There are different regulations, reporting and taxation requirements, which vary across the region. Therefore strong market due diligence, specific market knowledge and expertise in a changing environment are essential for success.[46]

Securities lending forms a growing part of the revenue of the prime brokerage arm of investment banks.

Securities lending is discussed further in Chapter 8.

Growth of CFD Market

Industry experts opine that a contract for difference (CFD) is one of the most innovative financial instruments that have been created since the 1990s. The proliferation in the use of CFDs, according to industry observers, is the reason for London's recent pre-eminence in terms of being a financial location for hedge traders. London has an edge over New York in this respect because CFDs are not allowed in the USA as a result of legal restrictions enforced by the regulators in the country.

According to one source, CFD was the brainchild of Brian Keelan and Jon Wood of the then UBS Warburg in the 1990s. In the beginning, they were used by institutional investors and hedge funds to limit exposure to volatility on the London Stock Exchange in a cost-effective manner. As well as being traded on margin, they aided in the avoidance of stamp duty, which is a government tax on the purchase and sale of securities.

Another source credits the development of CFDs to the derivatives desk of Smith New Court – a London-based trading firm in the 1990s. CFD enabled the

---

44 Short interest is the total number of shares of a particular stock that have been sold short by investors but have not yet been covered or closed out, which can be expressed as a number or as a percentage. When expressed as a percentage, short interest is the number of shorted shares divided by the number of shares outstanding. For example, a stock with 1.5 million shares sold short and 10 million shares outstanding has a short interest of 15% (1.5 million/ 10 million = 15%). (Investopedia)

45 A situation whereby an investor is forced to repurchase shares because the seller did not deliver the securities in a timely fashion, or did not deliver them at all.

46 RBC Dexia Investor Services (April 2007), Securities Lending Market Update.

firm's hedge fund clients to easily sell short in the market, i.e. the London Stock Exchange, with the benefit of leverage and the benefit from the associated stamp duty exemptions that were not available to outright share transactions. This also allowed them to avoid the need to borrow stock when they wanted to sell short.

Nowadays, they are one of the fastest growing areas in financial markets and make up an estimated 30% of all equities share dealing in the UK. CFDs which allow investors to "short" or sell a share, which is almost impossible in the ordinary share market, have been around since the 1980s, but were catapulted into the mainstream during the dot.com crash of 2000-2002. CFDs could have been invented for this scenario and some investors made a packet.[47]

Ever since then, CFDs have become mainstream financial products to the extent that investors have regularly used them to amass large stakes in corporations. According to industry watchers, the continuing liberation of capital markets that has created a fertile ground for the development of innovative new products has been credited for the success of CFDs since the 1990s. CFDs are now commonplace and their uses range from giving hedge funds cheap leverage to providing exposure to exotic equity sectors in emerging markets.

A CFD can be defined as an agreement between two parties to exchange, at the close of the contract, the difference between the opening price and closing price of the contract, with reference to the underlying share, multiplied by the number of shares specified within the contract. CFDs are not restricted to shares, but are also applicable to other assets such as bonds, commodities, foreign exchange and also to a portfolio of shares, such as an index.

The term "contract for difference" means that the product is cash-settled. There is no receipt or delivery of an underlying instrument, such as a share certificate. The result of the trade is the cash difference between the bought and sold price.

CFDs have many advantages over trading direct in financial assets including the following:

- Investors can buy exposure to financial assets for a fraction of the cost of buying the asset for real.
- As CFDs have become more accepted, the fees – or spread – taken by providers have been bid down by competition. That means CFDs are becoming a cheap source of leverage for hedge funds.
- Providers are now offering CFDs on an array of stocks, as opposed to only one or two.
- CFDs can help with pairs trading. If a hedge fund manager believes a company is undervalued compared to another then they can use CFDs to go long on the cheaper stock and go short on the dearer one.
- CFDs can be used to hedge positions and protect long-term holdings against

47 Hope, K. (13 May 2008), Contracts for Difference, City AM.

volatile market conditions. It is cheaper to open a short CFD position in shares rather than sell physical shares and then buy them back later.[48]

An interesting comment from the industry describes the Warren Buffer buy-and-hold investment model as "old school" when compared with the merits of the CFD, which allows for a wider spreading of cash as a result of the lack of securities holding.

The following example illustrates the advantage of a CFD with regard to the relatively low capital outlay required to profit from exposure to equities, for instance.

Supposing a hedge fund manager buys a CFD for 20,000 shares of pharmaceuticals firm Bizeneca that is currently trading at £1.50. The total value of their position would be £30,000. Interestingly, the initial margin, i.e. the deposit that needs to be put down equals £3,000, about 10% of the value of the position.

It is worth noting that margin requirements vary according to the liquidity of a particular stock and the level of perceived risk in the market at the time. In the event of high market volatility, margin requirement could rise to about 30%.

Of late, hedge funds have been using CFDs to invest in industry sectors – or hedge existing sector exposure – because there is no alternative in the capital markets.

Prime brokers have witnessed a recent trend whereby investors have been asking them to structure swaps, giving them exposure to a sector or index that the exchanges have not had the capacity to offer as listed derivatives.[49]

CFDs are currently traded in countries, apart from the UK, such as Germany, Italy, Switzerland, Norway, Sweden, Belgium, South Africa, Hong Kong, Singapore, France, Netherlands, Australia, New Zealand and the USA to non-residents only. Industry experts believe there will be expansion into new markets virtually every year. Waves, Turbo Certificates, and Callable Bull/Bear Contracts (CBBCs) are terms used to refer to CFDs on certain occasions.

The most popular use of CFDs is in Equity CFDs, i.e. CFDS on individual equities or shares. This type of CFD is typically available on shares traded on all European, North American and Asian Stock Markets.

The following is a simple illustration of an Equity CFD trade.

For this illustration a long trade, which is opened with a buy in the hope that the share price will go up, is used.

---

48 ibid.

49 A CFD can also be described as a derivative. The term derivative is very common and is used to describe any product that is based on an underlying instrument, i.e. a derivative of an underlying instrument.

Ess Telecom shares are currently trading 120–120.5.

A hedge fund, Biz Global Partners, has a hunch that the Ess Telecom share price is going to rise and places a trade to buy 500,000 shares as a CFD at 120.5p. The total value of the contract would be £602,500 but given the nature of CFD transactions, they would only need to make an initial 10% deposit, i.e. initial margin of £60,250.

The commission on the trade is £1,205 (£602,500 x 0.20%) and they do not have to pay any stamp duty as it is a CFD transaction.

A week later, Biz Global Partners' hunch is proved right and Ess Telecom shares rise to 125–125.5, and they make a decision to close their position by selling 500,000 Ess Telecom CFDs at 125p. The commission on the trade is £1,250 (£602,500 x 0.20%).

The profit on the trade is calculated thus:

Opening level	120.50p
Closing level	125.00p
Difference	4.50p
Profit on trade (4.5p x 500,000)	£22,500

Overall profit
The overall profit is calculated by taking into account the commission.

Profit on trade	£22,500
Commission	−£2,455
Overall profit on the trade	£20,045

In conclusion, CFDs are extraordinary business for investment banks and their prime brokerage divisions. Given that CFDs as derivative instruments can give an exposure to a company's share price without requiring the holder to buy the stock, it is not surprising that an increasing proportion of the equities traded in London are hedges for CFD positions.

Cross-Asset Prime Brokerage

This chapter discusses cross-asset prime brokerage with emphasis on foreign exchange and fixed income.

Introduction

The business model of prime brokerage is a model that lends itself to a number of asset classes. The flexibility to handle securities across asset classes is significant in prime brokerage, as in other areas of the financial markets. It is increasingly a distinguishing factor if a prime broker can provide high-quality execution and access across a broad asset class spectrum.

Cross-asset prime broking has become common in the industry and is driven by the ever-increasing volumes of business from the hedge fund sector. Hedge funds have been seeking multi-asset trading for some time, allowing them to apply their complex strategies across foreign exchange (FX), fixed income, options, futures and equities. In response, prime brokers are seeking to offer cross-product support to hedge funds as the industry develops.

While some prime brokers claim full asset class coverage, it is not the case for all prime brokers as the different parent investment banks of most prime brokers have developed their particular niches and expertise. Hence, there aren't many prime brokers who can meet the needs of all their hedge fund clients across asset classes. Even though they may have captured a significant share of the market, the top-tier players in the prime brokerage industry are known to specialise mainly in equity and equity derivatives prime broking, and their expertise in fixed income and futures is less well developed. However, experts believe a merger of divisions, for example the equity and fixed income desks, could provide cross-asset prime brokerage to hedge funds.

In this chapter, prime brokerage in two asset classes, foreign exchange and fixed income, will be discussed; the former in more depth than the latter.

Foreign Exchange

As seen in Chapter 5, foreign exchange prime brokerage is rising sharply. Foreign exchange prime brokerage provides a channel for its hedge fund clients, among others, to access liquidity at various executing dealers/brokers and at the same time maintain a credit relationship, place collateral and settle with a single entity, i.e. the prime broker.

Also shown in Chapter 5 is that the FX prime brokerage process entails a prime-broker client, such as a hedge fund, executing an FX trade with an executing dealer or broker[50] in the name of its prime broker (see Figure 7.1). As soon as the prime broker is alerted to and accepts the transaction by the client and executing dealer/broker, the prime broker, as opposed to the client, becomes the counterparty in the transaction with the executing dealer/broker. Additionally, the prime broker will concurrently enter into an offsetting transaction with the client. The responsibility for the confirmation and settlement of the trade (transaction) lies with both the prime broker and the executing dealer/

---

50 Also referred to as a "spoke bank" or "give-up" bank.

Figure 7.1 Prime Brokerage Transaction Flow

1. Client trades with executing dealer (for example, sells 100 USD/JPY).

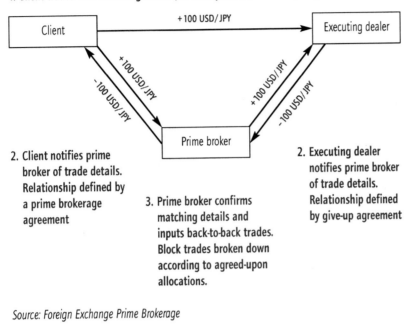

2. Client notifies prime broker of trade details. Relationship defined by a prime brokerage agreement

3. Prime broker confirms matching details and inputs back-to-back trades. Block trades broken down according to agreed-upon allocations.

2. Executing dealer notifies prime broker of trade details. Relationship defined by give-up agreement

Source: Foreign Exchange Prime Brokerage

broker, and at the same time the prime broker effects settlement with the client on a net basis. The prime broker usually charges the client a fee on a volume basis for the trades conducted in exchange for the privilege given to the client to trade in its name.

It is important to note that despite the contribution of the growth of hedge funds to the development of the prime brokerage business, the client base is quite varied. Apart from hedge funds, there are other clients such as commodity trading advisers (CTAs), pension funds, family offices, small banks and a host of others.

It is prudent at this stage to describe the FX trade process flow before delving further into the FX prime brokerage process.

FX Trade Process Flow

The FX trade process is represented diagrammatically in Figure 7.2. This diagram shows how each respective step in the FX trade process flow – pre-trade preparation, trade execution and capture, confirmation, netting, settlement and Nostro reconciliation – integrates with the other.

A brief description of each individual step is shown below.

Figure 7.2 FX Trade Process Flow

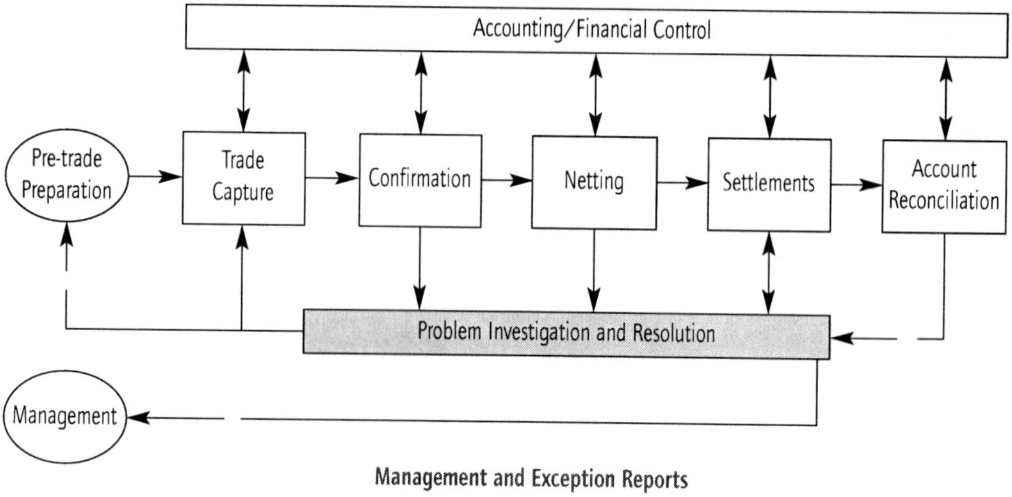

Accounting/Financial Control

Pre-trade Preparation → Trade Capture → Confirmation → Netting → Settlements → Account Reconciliation

Problem Investigation and Resolution

Management

Management and Exception Reports

Source: Foreign Exchange Transaction Processing

Pre-trade Preparation

This stage entails the agreement between the two parties involved in a trade on the procedures and practices required for execution of the trade in a safe and sound manner.

Trade Execution and Capture

This is the second phase of the process flow. It involves the transaction of the deal over a telephone line (the conversations are recorded) or via proprietary trading systems or multi-dealer systems. Trade data captured during this phase includes:

- trade date;
- time of execution;
- counterparty details;
- financial instrument traded, e.g. FX swaps, FX options and non-deliverable forwards;
- amount transacted;
- rate;
- settlement instructions.

Confirmation

This provides evidence of the terms of the FX transaction. There are a number of ways in which the confirmation process is handled in the FX markets. Counterparties in a spot, forward FX, or vanilla currency options transaction exchange electronic (via SWIFT) or paper confirmations that identify transaction details and provide relevant information.

A trade that has been confirmed between counterparties may be the subject of novation.[51]

Netting

This stage can be described as the sub-process whereby all trades that are due on a particular settlement date between two counterparties are combined and calculated as a single payment in each currency. This is known in the industry as bilateral netting. If a bilateral netting agreement is not in place, payment instructions are sent to a Nostro bank for all the amounts owed plus expected receipts. The usual practice is to send standard settlement instructions (SSIs) one day before settlement date, depending on the currency's settlement requirements.

Settlement

This stage is where payments are exchanged between counterparties on the value date of the transaction in accordance with the SSIs. Settlement instructions should contain the following information, presented as clearly as possible:

- the recipient's account name, account address, and account number;
- the name of the receiving bank, a SWIFT/ISO address, and a branch identifier;
- the identity of any intermediary bank used by the recipient.

Account Reconciliation

This activity takes place at the end of the settlement process in order to ensure that a trade has been settled properly and all cash flows have happened. It is the process whereby expected and actual cash are reconciled. Both counterparties usually commence reconciliation once they receive notification from their respective settlement bank.

Account reconciliation is an important process which ensures that mismatches in the expect cash movements and the actual movements are uncovered in a timely manner in a firm's currency accounts. The reason for the cash breaks might be that wrong settlement or trade information was captured or that an error occurred during the payment process.

After successful reconciliation, the account and control function of a firm makes certain that FX deals are properly recorded on the balance sheet and income statement in the general ledger.

Accounting entries are initially booked after the inception of the trade. At the end of each trade date, all sub-ledger accounts flow to the general ledger. If there are discrepancies, they should be investigated as soon as possible to make certain that the firm's books and records are accurate. It is the responsi-

---

51 This involves exchange of new debt or obligations for the ones that are older and still in use.

bility of the accounting function to ensure that outstanding positions are constantly marked-to-market until close-out.[52] After this, realised gains and losses are calculated and reported.

Cash-flow movements that occur on the settlement date are also posted to the general ledger in agreement with the conventions of accounting procedures. The receipt and payment of expected cash flows at settlement are calculated in a firm's operation system.

FX Prime Brokerage Deal Process

The prime brokerage deal process flow occurs in essentially four steps.

1. Notification

Once a trade has been executed by the executing dealer, the client and the executing dealer inform the prime broker of the material terms of the deal. The material terms of an FX transaction to be transmitted to the prime broker depend on the type of the transaction. For example, for a spot trade these terms include:

- transaction date;
- settlement date;
- amount of each currency to be delivered to each party;
- the buying party;
- the selling party.

On the other hand, for an FX option the material terms include:

- amounts of each currency;
- strike price;
- type of FX option transaction (e.g. European or American);
- premium;
- expiration date;
- any other term that is deemed important in the market.

Once the prime broker receives notification of a trade, it has the right and obligation to either accept or reject the trade depending on whether the trade fulfils the conditions of the prime brokerage and give-up agreements. The following are reasons for which a prime broker may reject a trade that has been given up:

- The trade is not within specified credit limits.
- The trade is not an allowable transaction type as stipulated in the give-up agreement with the executing dealer.

---

52 This is a process whereby a current long or short position is eliminated or reduced by making an opposite transaction of the same security. Also known as offset.

- The trade is not specified within the stipulated tenor (i.e. the term or life of a contract) limits.
- There is a mismatch between the trade details provided by the executing dealer and the client.

2. Matching and Acceptance or Rejection

A bilateral agreement between the prime broker and the client, and the prime broker and the executing dealer typically define the standards and procedures governing the notification of trade details and the acceptance or rejection of trades. Traditionally, notifications from the executing dealer to the prime broker are completed in a timely manner. It is the notification from the client or executing dealer that is, however, inconsistent and can therefore affect the timing of the acceptance or rejection by the prime broker.

3. Confirmation

As soon as a prime broker successfully matches and accepts a trade, separate confirmations are exchanged between both a) the prime broker and the executing dealer and b) the prime broker and the client, to provide legal evidence of the terms of the transaction. Confirmations play an important role in the systematic functioning of the marketplace, given that they reduce the market risk and losses that originate from settlement errors. Included in the transaction confirmation are all relevant items of data that permit the two counterparties in the trade to concur on the terms of the trade in an accurate manner. Additionally, all relevant settlement instructions for each deal are categorised in each transaction.

4. Allocation

This involves the prime broker splitting accepted trades into smaller amounts and allocating them to specific underlying funds or counterparties. In some cases, an agent may carry out trades on behalf of counterparties and pass them on to the prime broker for allocation.

Evolution of Prime-brokered Trade Execution

It is well known in the financial markets that the prime-brokered trade execution model has evolved in recent times. Traditionally, FX prime-brokered transactions were instigated manually by the client. In this scenario, the client assumes the name of the prime broker when trading and uses the prime broker's credit line with the executing dealer. The execution of transactions involves direct communication between the client and executing dealer, in which the identities of both parties are known.

In more recent times, prime brokers have been leveraging the benefits of electronic communication networks and electronic broking platforms to provide trade execution. These platforms allow for automated program trading, which usually involves the use of an application programming interface (API) that provides access to executable prices by way of a two-way message interface between the foreign exchange market and a client's internal trading infrastructure. Remarkably, at the time of execution, there is normally no identification of the trade as being prime-brokered in the electronic prime-broker model as the executing dealer only sees the name of the prime broker. The client is provided with an element of anonymity as its identity is not known to the executing dealer.

Value Proposition

Value proposition is the benefit that an end-user gets from a service, the thing that convinces them to engage the services of the provider. In essence, it consists of the sum total of benefits which a provider promises that a client will receive in return for the customer's associated payment (or other value-transfer).

It is expressed in the marketing field as:

Value proposition = What the client gets for what the client pays

Accordingly, a client can evaluate a prime broker's value proposition on two broad dimensions with multiple subsets:

1. Relative performance: what the client derives from the prime broker relative to a competitor's offering.
2. Price: which consists of the payment the client makes to acquire the bundle of services from the prime broker, plus the access cost.

Benefit to the Client

One of the major benefits of FX prime brokerage to the client is that it allows it to maximise its credit relationship and activities and at the same improve efficiency. Prime brokerage also streamlines the credit and documentation process since the client is subject to one internal credit review and executes one master trading agreement and credit support annex with the prime broker as opposed to a number of agreements with multiple dealers. The use of a prime brokerage agreement allows for the more efficient use of collateral for margin relationship. In addition, the client needs to manage one credit relationship to achieve trading relationships with more than one counterparty and net margin. Furthermore, the client can access pricing and liquidity from a greater number of dealers and potentially widen the scope of its activities.

Another benefit to the client is the ability to consolidate positions and improve execution. For instance, a client may create a foreign exchange position with a number of different counterparties, which are then consolidated into a single position with the prime broker.

This single position is easier for the client to manage than individual positions with a variety of counterparties. Additionally, FX prime brokerage provides the client with a greater liquidity that enables it to execute larger FX trades.

Benefit to the Prime Broker

The principal benefit for the prime broker is the fee-based revenue stream it generates from the bundle of products it offers to its clients; a boon in an age when foreign exchange spreads continue to narrow.

Prime brokerage offers efficiencies of scale in regard to transaction processing and technology investment and allows an investment bank to leverage its technology and operating infrastructure. Given that execution is continually migrating to electronic platforms, investment banks see prime brokerage as a chance to build a fee-based business into their electronic foreign-exchange platform in order to recoup their investment in the platform.

Benefit to the Executing Dealer

Increased execution flows coupled with the ability to transact business with counterparties that would normally require credit enhancement are some of the benefits that executing dealers derive from FX prime brokerage.

Legal Frameworks and Agreements

The legal framework for a prime broker encompasses the establishment of a prime brokerage agreement which requires explicit legal documents that express the rights and responsibilities of the client, prime broker and executing dealers. The give-up agreement is used by the foreign exchange prime broker to document its relationship with the executing dealer, while the prime brokerage agreement documents the relationship between the foreign exchange prime broker and the client.

Give-up Agreement

This is the agreement between the executing dealer and the prime broker whereby the prime broker agrees to assume the role of the counterparty to each transaction executed by the client with the executing dealer, conditional on compliance with the specified terms. A give-up agreement is essential when a client designated by a prime broker executes transactions with an executing dealer that are "given-up" to the prime broker. The result is one transaction between the dealer and the prime broker, and an offsetting transaction between the prime broker and the designated party, or funds or accounts for which that party executes foreign exchange trades. In practice, a give-up agreement is routinely executed as a master agreement complemented by a give-up agreement notice for each prime-broker client that will execute trades with the relevant executing dealer. In the give-up agreement notice, details of the client are specified and allowable products, tenors and specific limits that apply to the trades that the prime broker will accept for that client are also included. There are similarities between the terms specified in the give-up agreement and those in the prime brokerage agreement (see below), and in some cases the terms are identical. However, as these terms are specified in the give-up agreement notice, the executing dealer can then determine, before executing any trade with the prime broker's client, the obligation of the prime broker in accepting the give-up of the transaction. In some circumstances, the prime broker may be contacted by the executing dealer to request acceptance of trades that may be outside the limit stipulated in the agreements.

The Master FX Give-Up Agreement published by the Foreign Exchange Committee (FXC)[53] is used by market participants for documenting foreign exchange give-up relationships. According to the Foreign Exchange Committee: *"The Master FX Give-Up Agreement is to be entered into by the prime broker and an executing dealer. The bilateral nature of the Master FX Give-Up Agreement reflects the need for efficiency and standardisation and takes into account the fact that a prime broker may designate a number of clients to engage in foreign exchange give-up transactions on its behalf pursuant to a single master agreement."*

Prime Brokerage Agreement

This agreement may stipulate that when a prime broker agrees to enter into foreign exchange transactions with dealers approved by the prime broker, it is the prime broker as opposed to the client that will become party to these transactions, provided that the relevant terms specified in the prime brokerage agreement are met.

There are usually two types of terms as follows:

- Each transaction will have allowable products, such as spot, forward, or option transactions, and a tenor that does not exceed a specified minimum.
- The transaction will have to be within specified limits, which may include settlement, open position limit, or both.

These limits typically apply to the total of all transactions executed by the client with an executing dealer and are normally either specified in the prime brokerage agreement or communicated to the prime client by the prime broker in order that the client is aware of them at all times.

It should be noted that there are terms and conditions contained in the prime brokerage agreement that are outside the scope of this book.

Compensation Agreement

In this agreement there are provisions for the compensation of losses in the event that the give-up of a transaction is not accepted by the prime broker. It is usually executed in conjunction with the Master FX Give-Up Agreement.

---

53 The Foreign Exchange Committee is convened by the Federal Reserve Bank of New York and is composed of representatives from major financial institutions in the foreign exchange markets.

Credit Risk Mitigation

The tri-party framework of the prime brokerage model has an added dimension of complexity with respect to the requirements for prime brokerage arrangements to include credit-limit monitoring against the limit laid down in the governing legal arrangements. The execution of a trade by an executing dealer and the acceptance of a transaction should be contingent on approval of credit lines for a client as well as availability.

The following are some of the credit risk mitigating practices of prime brokers:

- Prime brokers do not typically finalise a trade without confirming sufficient availability under the give-up line. Give-up line usage information is updated once a deal is accepted by the prime broker and it is usually made accessible to prime brokerage service personnel, risk managers and executing dealers.
- Prime brokers implement real-time credit systems to actively monitor open positions against limits and pending give-up trades.
- The sales area of a prime broker assesses its credit exposure to a client in a timely manner and its systems automatically update a client's credit status as soon as a trade is accepted by the prime broker.
- Prime brokers have policies and procedures to address credit-limit breaches and document the approval of limit exceptions. Reports of credit-line excesses and exceptions are produced on a regular basis for review.

Executing dealers also mitigate credit risk by using appropriate tools to monitor open positions and limits against pending trades. If such tools were used with straight-through processing features for the acceptance and processing of trades, it could promote efficiencies, especially at a time when volumes observed in the foreign exchange markets are on the increase.

Fixed Income

Introduction

Any type of investment that yields a regular (or fixed) return is generally referred to as fixed income. There is a contrast between fixed income securities and variable return securities such as stocks in that fixed income securities are sold to investors to raise funds to finance an organisation's ongoing operations and in return the investors are paid regular interest on their funds and repaid the principal on the bond at maturity. Equities, on the other hand, involve pledging a stake (giving equity) in the organisation.

Fixed income securities are popularly known as bonds. The reason for this name is that at the time of the purchase of a basic bond, the amount of income and the timing of the payments are known to the purchaser. Fixed income is also called debt instruments and debentures as well.

The following are the most widely known characteristics of bonds:

- **Time to maturity** – This is the date the issuer will make a lump sum payment to return the principal, which eliminates the debt.
- **Principal, par value, face value** – These are three names for the same item, the amount that is returned to the bondholder at maturity.
- **Coupon** – The interest payment that will be made to the bondholder.

It should be noted that the principal may or may not be the price the purchaser paid for the bond. Depending on the timing of the purchase of the bond, the purchaser may pay more or less than the par value. Often, bonds are sold below par when they are issued, i.e. they are sold at a "discount".

Fixed Income Prime Brokerage

There are variations in the prime broker service offerings in the fixed income market among broker dealers and their clients with respect to service agreements, products traded, means of communication and automation. There is also diversity among the types of hedge funds and asset managers that make use of prime brokerage services and their trading strategies as well as their business practices.

The prime broker is hired by the client to perform essential back-office functions such as receipt and delivery of fixed income securities on the client's behalf with the executing dealer that executed the trade of fixed income instruments. The client of such a hedge fund is not restricted to transacting fixed income business with one specific prime broker, but rather with a number of prime brokers depending on the firm's preference. This may include, but is not limited to, the trading desk of the prime broker.

If the executing dealer is part of the same organisation as the prime broker, it must maintain a "Chinese Wall" between the prime brokerage operation and the trading desk. This separation should include technology, research and operations departments.

Products Traded

Depending on the terms of the agreement between a prime broker and a client, all types of fixed income instruments can be traded including:

- plain vanilla debt securities;
- futures;
- repos;
- interest rate swaps;
- mortgage-backed securities.

International securities are often traded and they raise cross-border settlement issues. Foreign exchange transactions are frequently required to support the fixed income transaction. Other transactions could be structured as a combination of a straight fixed income trade with one counterparty that is then leveraged with a repo or securities lending agreement with another counterparty. The complexity involved in the range of transactions has led to thoroughness on the part of prime brokers when tracking trades on behalf of their prime brokerage clients.

As in other asset classes, in order to effectively manage the settlement process the prime broker need to be informed of the details of a client's trade at the earliest point in the transaction cycle, irrespective of the simplicity or complexity of the transaction.

Client–Executing Dealer relations

A hedge fund manager (the client) executing a trade usually shops for a fair bid or offer price on securities they intend to sell or purchase. Hence, especially in the fixed income markets where counterparties routinely negotiate the terms of a trade, the hedge fund exercises the right to conduct business with several executing dealers.

Block Trade Execution and Sub-account Breakdowns

As soon as a trade has been completed between the hedge fund and the executing dealer at the block level, the hedge fund will often provide the dealer with a list of sub-accounts for which the trade was done. This process is often called "allocation" or "breakdowns".[54] Each one of the sub-accounts could probably appoint a different clearing agent (this can be a custodial bank or a prime broker) to process their portion of the block trade. It is the responsibility of the executing dealer to process trades for each sub-account through its books and records, and to coordinate settlement with each sub-account's appointed agents (either custodian or prime broker).

Timing of Allocations and Settlement Instructions

When the block trade is executed between a hedge fund and the executing dealer, the executing dealer is often not informed that a prime broker may possibly be involved in the transaction. The evidence of the existence of a prime brokerage relationship is only revealed when the executing dealer receives the allocations from the hedge fund and the executing dealer's system performs a check on an internal database for standing settlement instructions for the sub-account. Some hedge funds communicate the mandate for handling and clearing to the executing dealer at the time of trade execution.

The speed at which an executing dealer is able to advise the prime broker of the details of a trade are impacted by the speed at which the hedge fund provides it with the sub-account allocations. Timeliness of allocations is less of an issue in an age where straight-through processing is commonplace.

Client–Prime Broker Relations

In some cases, the executing dealer is informed of the sub-account breakdown after the details of the trade for a sub-account that the prime broker clears and

---

54 There may also be occasions when a block trade is done with a hedge fund and sub-account breakdowns are not involved.

105

settles are communicated to the prime broker. The reverse of this sequence of events is also possible, depending on the speed at which the hedge fund communicates the details of the trade or sub-account to the prime broker.

Methods of Communication

Communication methods that hedge funds use to inform their prime brokers of the details of trades that they will clear and settle differ according to the size of the firm. While some larger hedge funds utilise automated order management systems (OMS) or trading systems, the smaller hedge funds utilise electronic spreadsheets or faxed trade tickets. The communication of the messages could be in real time or in batch, either intra-day or end-of-day in the case of the hedge funds that generate messages using OMS, or once or twice a day for those that use spreadsheets.

Some hedge funds have chosen the more cost-effective method of using push technology provided by the executing dealer that involves direct trade input by the hedge fund managers into a dedicated screen displayed via a web browser. It should be noted that apart from the automated messages generated by an OMS or trading system, there is a time-lag between trade execution with the executing dealer and the time of submission of the trade to the prime broker by the hedge fund.

Trade Information for Sub-accounts

Trade information communicated by the hedge fund to the prime broker for each trade executed for a sub-account includes:

- identifier of the sub-account(s);
- identification of the executing dealer;
- trade date;
- settlement date;
- unique security identifier, e.g. ISIN, CUSIP;
- quantity traded;
- price;
- yield;
- currency;
- accrued interest;
- total net money;
- reference transaction codes generated by either the hedge fund manager's or executing dealer's systems that prime brokers use for reference;
- settlement instructions;
- unique codes that link the trade to other associated trades such as multi-leg or derivative transactions.

Executing Dealer–Prime Broker Relations

A manual matching process characterises the relations between the executing dealer and the prime broker. It involves a prime broker, when informed of a trade by the hedge manager, telephoning an executing dealer to reconcile the details of the trade. In some other cases, the executing dealer will contact the prime broker about a trade before the hedge fund has advised the prime broker about it. The verbal communication over the phone will entail exchange of trade details, including the information referenced above, between the prime broker and the executing broker.

Discrepancies usually occur between the information supplied by the hedge fund to the prime broker and that provided by the executing dealer, but it is the responsibility of the prime broker to get in touch with the hedge fund in order to resolve the differences.

Securities Lending

This chapter discusses the concept of securities lending, which is an important part of the prime brokerage service offering. Also included is a discussion on the types of risk in securities lending and associated controls.

Introduction

Securities lending is a major component of the prime brokerage business. The scale of the securities lending facility that prime brokers offer to hedge funds depends on the strategies that these funds pursue. Two strategies that depend heavily on securities borrowing are long/short equity and convertible arbitrage.

Securities lending involves the temporary exchange of securities, usually for other securities or cash of an equivalent value (or occasionally a mixture of cash and securities), with an obligation to redeliver a like quantity of the same securities at a future date.

There are two persistent issues that experts believe come with securities lending – one operational, the other systemic. First, there is always the risk of borrower default, which most prime brokers believe can be managed with prudent polices. The second issue is more persistent and harder for prime brokers to dispel – the effect of shorting securities on driving down asset prices.

Nevertheless, securities lending is a major revenue earner for prime brokers as hedge fund demand seems insatiable.

Definition of Securities Lending

Defining securities lending would appear to be straightforward, but in some ways the term is misleading and some experts believe it is factually incorrect. In a number of jurisdictions, the transaction commonly described as "securities lending" should be defined as:

"A transaction that involves the disposal (or sale) of securities linked to the subsequent reacquisition of equivalent securities by means of an agreement."

Another definition of securities lending from a prime brokerage perspective is:

"When a prime broker lends securities owned by its clients to short sellers, allowing the prime broker to create additional revenue (commissions) on the short sale transaction."

Securities lending transactions are collateralised and all aspects of the transaction are dealt with using the terms agreed between the parties involved.

History of Securities Lending from 1990s

Today, securities lending and borrowing have become an integral part of securities markets. Without them, market liquidity and settlement efficiency would be greatly reduced. The history of the securities market dates back to the development of securities trading markets. Industry sources believe that events in the UK in the 20th century, whereby specialist intermediaries sourced gilts for the jobbers or market makers, were the building blocks for the securities lending market of recent times.

During this era, collateral, usually non-cash, was exchanged between these parties at the end of the trading day and provided protection for the lenders. This allowed the practice of "bond-washing"[55] to take place and was a predecessor to tax arbitrage, i.e. trading that takes advantage of a difference in tax rates or tax systems as the basis for profit.

1990s

In the 1990s, securities lending became very popular in most markets. Notable activities in these markets included the following:

- There was an increasing demand for securities borrowing with a view to supporting hedging and trading strategies.
- During this decade, increased computer processing power, access to real-time prices and automated trade execution were harnessed to devise new trading strategies like statistical arbitrage.
- The fall of Long-Term Capital Management in the latter years of this decade did not affect the growth of hedge funds under management.
- Investment banks, in a bid to support the activities of the growing hedge fund industry, built global prime brokerage operations.
- The sharp increase in the US short-term interest rates in 1994 resulted in losses for many securities lenders who had taken US-dollar cash as collateral and were reinvesting it in a variety of money market instruments. These securities lenders learned their lesson and, as a result, improved their risk management procedures and devised clear reinvestment guidelines.
- During the 1990s, many regulatory, tax and structural barriers were removed throughout the world.
- Between 1997 and 1998, when the East Asian financial crises[56] gripped most of Asia, the authorities in a number of countries imposed regulations on short selling, drawing a link with currency speculation.

2000s

This decade has also witnessed a further growth in securities lending volumes and key trends include the following:

- The market is increasingly segmented, with the emergence of specialist regional players and third-party securities lending agents.
- Continuing deregulations and tax changes are making the establishment of new securities lending markets possible in countries like Brazil, India, Korea and Taiwan.

---

55 This is the situation whereby a bond holder sells a security with interest and buys it back after the coupon is paid so as to convert the interest income into a capital gain.

56 These crises were kicked off by the decision of the Thai government to float the baht, resulting in its collapse.

- In 2002 and 2003, there were few Initial Public Offerings (IPOs) and Mergers and Acquisitions (M&A) opportunities and hence there was a slow-down in the growth of equity stock lending. There was, however, the development of traded credit, and corporate bond markets encouraged growth in the fixed income sector.
- Tax arbitrage opportunities are disappearing in the wake of tax harmonisation.
- New transaction types are emerging, such as:
  - contracts for difference (CFD);
  - total return swaps;
  - equity repo.

Reasons for Borrowing Securities

Prime brokers borrow securities to support their hedge fund clients and are deliberately secretive about it, given their desire to protect their hedge fund clients' trading strategy and motivation.

Some of the reasons behind the borrowing of securities are to:

- transfer ownership temporarily for the benefit of both lender and borrower (dividend reinvestment plan arbitrage, tax arbitrage and so on);
- partly finance transactions inspired by the desire to lend cash;
- cover a short position (arbitrage trading, naked shorting and settlement coverage).

Arbitrage Trading
Borrowing for this purpose is to cover a short position in one security that has been obtained to hedge a long position in another with a view to executing an arbitrage strategy.

Naked Shorting
This is defined as the practice of selling securities short without first borrowing the shares or ensuring that the shares can be borrowed. The expectation is that these securities can be bought back at a lower price in order to return them to the lender. Industry experts opine that it is an illegal practice because it contravenes the conventional borrowing of securities, or determining that they can be borrowed, before they are sold short. This has given manipulators a chance to force prices of securities down, disregarding normal stock supply/demand patterns.

Settlement Coverage
Efficient settlement can be achieved by borrowing securities to avert settlement failure and has provided the necessary impetus for many securities depositories, such as custody banks, to enter into the automated securities lending business. This allows them to compensate clients automatically for making their securities

available for borrowing by the depository, with a view to avoiding any settlement failures.

The Transaction Life Cycle

The following describes the typical structure of a securities lending transaction. This description assumes the format of a basic manual transaction that does not take into account the adoption of straight-through processing. This is because straight-through processing (STP) is implemented in a variety of ways and, to maintain simplicity, it is beneficial to describe a manual process.

Trade Execution

Before a trade is executed, the counterparties make decisions on the legal agreement that will cover the transaction. If a central counterparty is not used for the transaction, the onus is on each counterparty to check the credit quality of the other, ensuring that the counterparty risk can be assessed and the pricing of the trade is accurate.

The parties to the transaction establish the securities that are eligible for borrowing, maturity, pricing, collateral eligibility and necessary margins. These elements are described as follows:

- **Maturity** – Security loans are largely made on a open basis, such that loans can be returned or reset, either on demand or following an agreed notice period that is usually between one and three days.
- **Transaction size** – While it is widely recognised that definitive figures are not available, one thing is for sure: average transaction sizes vary between markets. Transaction sizes in securities-driven trades (usually equity loans) are smaller than in cash-driven trades (usually government securities) – in some markets about a tenth of the size.
- **Pricing** – Payment, i.e. compensation to the lender, is agreed at the beginning of the transaction and is normally by fee for a securities loan and through repo rate under repo.
- **Collateralisation** – As stated before, the borrower is usually required to pledge collateral in the form of cash, securities and standby letters of credit. If the lender and borrower agree on a standby letter of credit to be used as collateral, the borrower will require a bank to provide a letter of credit for a specified amount and the lender will make available the securities for a period during which this amount exceeds a predetermined fraction of their market value. The lender now has a right to draw down the letter of credit as soon as the borrower is in default on its payment obligations.

  In certain jurisdictions, government regulations specify the type of collateral that lenders can accept, especially if the lenders are fund managers. Some jurisdictions prevent some types of funds from accepting foreign securities or securities not denominated in their local currency.

  Credit standing is a criterion that borrowers use to determine the type of collateral that they offer to lenders. A prime broker that is part of a highly rated bank will seek to offer cash, which it can raise inexpensively, while an A-rated prime broker, for instance, might find it less expensive to provide a letter of credit and a less highly rated one may choose to provide equity from its own inventory.

- **Haircuts and margins** – Lenders usually request margin to supplement the value of the assets loaned to the borrower. Margin may be imposed as a reduction in the valuation of the collateral taken (haircut) and as an increase in the collateral required relative to the value of securities or cash lent, i.e. the initial margin.

  At this stage it would be beneficial to define the following terms:

  - **Haircut** – This is a percentage that is deducted from the par value of the assets that are being used as collateral. The value of the haircut reflects the perceived risk associated with holding the assets. For example, government bonds (which are seen as fairly safe) might have a haircut of 1%, while for a stock option (which is seen as less safe) the haircut might be as high as 30%. According to Investopedia, the term haircut comes from the fact that market makers can trade at such a thin spread.

  - **Initial margin** – When counterparties pledge collateral whose market value is equal to that of the cash or securities they have borrowed, they must pay initial margin. It is typically related to the price volatility of the securities borrowed.

  - **Variation margin** – Variation margin or maintenance margin is not collateral, but a daily offsetting of profits and losses necessitated by the adjusted value of the collateral in relation to the market value of the borrowed securities or cash falling below a certain level.

  The following formula[57] describes the relationship between the initial margin and haircuts:

  $$(1+m)\,s \le (1-h)\,c$$

  Where m = initial margin, s = market value of securities loaned, h = haircut and c = market value of collateral taken.

  In theory, the scale of margin requirements may be dependent on the quality, liquidity and price volatility of the securities lent, the creditworthiness of the counterparty, the term of the loan or the frequency with which collateral will be revalued and margin calls made.

- **Confirmation** – Confirmation of the economic and legal terms of the securities loan is the next step after the transaction has been executed. These confirmations are communicated usually through SWIFT messages on the day of the trade, given that borrowers seek possession of the borrowed securities within a shorter settlement cycle than for an outright securities sale.

57 Source: International Organisation of Securities Commissions and Bank for International Settlements (1999). Securities Lending Transactions: Market Development and Implications.

These terms include securities of the funds involved, the price, the type of collateral, the margin requirement, the settlement date and the counterparty. Also included are material changes during the term of the transaction that are agreed between the parties as they happen and may also be confirmed if either party wishes it. Examples of material changes are collateral adjustments or collateral substitution. Any mismatches between firms' respective confirmations will be detected and the confirmations will be reconciled and reissued. The loan confirmation process is usually performed on a bilateral basis directly between the counterparties of the trade.

- **Clearing** – Once loan matching and confirmation have taken place then the stage is set for clearing; that is, the calculation of the delivery or payment obligation on the settlement date. According to industry experts, the use of netting arrangements, whether bilateral or multilateral, prior to the settlement of transactions is rare. Once the obligations of the counterparties have been confirmed, settlement instructions are transmitted to the settlement system.
- **Settlement** – This process kicks off with the initial delivery of securities from the lender to the borrower and in most cases a transfer of collateral from borrower to lender. The next step is the transmission of the instructions to transfer the securities and funds to the entity that is operating the settlement systems required to discharge the obligations. Most prime brokers settle through Central Securities Depositories (CSDs). To complete the settlement process of the initial delivery, irrevocable and unconditional transfers on the books of the CSD should indicate the delivery of the loaned security and the corresponding collateral. In order to effectively cancel a securities lending transaction, both borrower and lender have to mutually agree that as long as the initial loan has not been settled, the instructions can be rescinded with confidence that the subsequent settlement will not occur.

There are a number of methods used for settlement, depending on the type of collateral that the borrower presented and the settlement entity or entities, and they are as follows:

- Delivery versus payment (DVP) – This is a procedure in which the buyer's payment for securities is due at the time of delivery. Security delivery and payment are simultaneous.
- Delivery versus delivery (DVD) – This is the transfer of securities from the account of the lender to the account of the borrower for payment at the time of the purchase of other securities, simultaneously with the transfer of such other securities.
- Free-of-payment (FOP) – This is the transfer of collateral from one holder to another holder free of payment, i.e. the final delivery of collateral before the transfer of borrowed funds or securities.

In most cases, the settlement procedure is the same for the two legs of the deal. That is to say, if the first leg of the transaction takes place on a DVP basis then the second leg will also take place on a DVP basis.

In most settlement systems, securities loans are settled as FOP deliveries and the collateral is taken separately, possibly in a different payment or settlement system and perhaps a different country and time zone. For instance,

UK equities might be lent against collateral provided by a European International Central Securities Depository or US dollar cash collateral paid in New York. This can result in what is known in the securities market as "daylight exposure", a period during which the loan is not covered as the lent securities have been delivered but the collateral securities have not yet been received. To avoid this exposure, some lenders insist on pre-collateralisation, therefore transferring the exposure to the borrower.[58]

Figure 8.1 Delivery versus payment settlement scheme

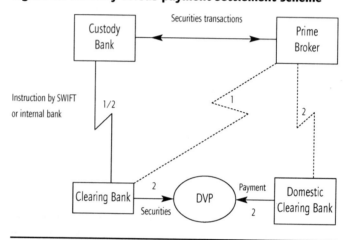

Note: 1 and 2 represent settlement options described as:

1. Internal, if the same clearing house manages accounts for both prime broker (buyer) and custody bank (seller);
2. External, when the clearing house delivers securities in exchange for funds.

- **Settlement period** – One of the key characteristics of a securities loan transaction is that the settlement of the initial delivery of the loaned securities and pledged collateral is achieved in a shorter cycle than settlement of an outright purchase transaction for the same market. The convention for the settlement interval in some securities lending/repo markets is T+0 while in most lending markets it is T+1. It should be noted that these intervals are indicative of market convention as opposed to the settlement system's capability. This shorter settlement life cycle highlights the purposes of securities lending, for instance to avoid settlement failure on outright trades, to provide immediate liquidity and to support short selling. Industry convention suggests that there is no true forward security lending market.

58 Source: "An Introduction to Securities Lending" © Mark C. Faulkner.

However, some lenders are willing to lend securities for settlement several days or weeks in the future.

- **Inter-settlement events** – On completion of the initial leg of the loan/repo, certain events require management through the life cycle of the loan to guarantee loan performance and to mitigate participants' risk exposure to each other. The lender is entitled to all of the economic benefits akin to those linked with beneficial ownership of the loaned securities and the borrower is entitled to the same for any securities pledged as collateral. These benefits include:
  - amounts equal to cash and stock dividends;
  - interest payments;
  - stock splits;
  - rights of distributions;
  - conversion privileges.

The onus is on each party to the deal to therefore track these events and make manufactured payments (i.e. substitute payments) in lieu of these events.

Over the course of the life of the loan, the borrower has to maintain the value of the collateral held in relation to that of the cash or securities on loan, in accordance with the terms of the contract between the parties in the transaction. As a consequence, the borrower revalues these holdings (collateral and loaned securities) at current market prices, i.e. marking-it-to-market on a daily basis. Both borrower and lender normally perform this process and must concur on price sources, preferably real-time information feeds that would also aid in the tracking of exposures.

- **Settlement of return leg** – This is the final step in the securities lending transaction. As for securities-driven transactions, the borrower would have to transfer the same securities that were borrowed, or equivalent securities, to the lender and the lender, in turn, would return the collateral provided by the borrower.
- **Termination of the loan** – As most securities loans are open (explanation provided later in the chapter) they may be terminated by the lender recalling securities or the borrower returning them. The borrower will typically return borrowed securities once it has filled its short position. A borrower may opt for refinancing its loan positions by borrowing more cheaply from other lenders and returning securities to the original lender.

Different Types of Securities Lending Transactions

Most securities lending transactions are collateralised, either with other securities or with cash deposits. This is to protect the lender against the possible default of the borrower. When lenders are offered securities as collateral, the borrower has to pay a fee to the lender. However, when they are given cash as collateral, they pay the borrower interest but at a rate that is lower than market rates, so that they can reinvest the cash and make a return. Negotiation now takes place between these parties and normally takes into account factors like supply and demand for the particular securities, collateral flexibility, the size of any manufactured dividend and the likelihood of the lender recalling the securities early.

Transaction Structures

Securities lending transactions are usually structured in one of three ways:

- securities loan transactions;
- repurchase agreements;
- sell–buy back arrangement.

While the legal structure of these transactions differs, the economics are similar, given that there is a temporary exchange of securities, typically for cash or collateral.

Securities loan transactions

In a typical securities loan transaction, a lender such as a custody bank lends securities to a prime broker, which becomes contractually obligated to redeliver a like quantity of the same security (see Figure 8.2). Securities borrowers are generally required to provide collateral to assure the performance of their redelivery obligation. Collateral may take the form of cash, other securities or a bank-issued letter of credit.

The following is a list of types of collateral:

- government bonds issued by G7, G10 or non-G7 governments;
- corporate bonds of various credit ratings;
- convertible bonds – matched or unmatched to the securities being lent;
- certificates of deposits drawn on institutions of a specified credit quality;
- warrants that are matched or unmatched to securities being lent;
- equities of specified indices;
- letters of credit from banks of a specified quality;
- delivery by value (DBV) – both concentrated and unconcentrated and of a certain asset class;
- other money market instruments.

It is standard industry practice for the lender of securities to receive initial margin from the prime broker that is collateral in excess of the market value of the loaned securities. This acts as a buffer against an adverse change in the price of loaned securities relative to collateral in the event that the borrower, i.e. the prime broker, defaults on its return obligation. The lender receives a fee that is negotiated at the time of the transaction. Loans can be made, an open (terminable on demand) or term basis.

The lender usually does not retain legal title to the securities that are lent. The prime broker obtains full title to the securities. The transaction would not be viable if the lender keeps legal title to the securities it has lent, since the prime broker may need legal title to the securities to transfer them to another party. Even if the prime broker defaults on its delivery obligation, the lender has no property interest in the original securities that could be asserted against any person to whom the hedge fund may have transferred them. The lender's protection is its right to foreclose on the collateral.[59]

Transaction collateralised with assets other than cash

Figure 8.2 Securities loan transaction (borrow vs pledge of securities)

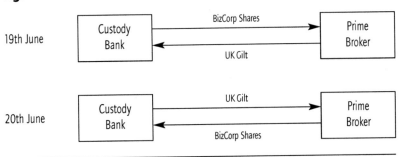

Example 1: The following is an illustration of a securities loan transaction against collateral other than cash.

A prime broker borrows 500,000 shares from a custody bank and pledges UK gilts. The custody bank charges a lending fee of 50 basis points for 1 day from 19 June to 20 June 2008.

The return to the custody bank against collateral other than cash derives from the fee charged to the prime broker. The cash flow for this transaction reads as follows:

- **Transaction date:** 19 June 2008
- **Settlement date:** 20 June 2008
- **Term:** Open[60]
- **Security:** BizCorp
- **Security price:** £10 per share
- **Quantity:** 50,000 shares
- **Loan value:** £500,000.00
- **Lending fee:** 50 basis points
- **Collateral:** UK gilts
- **Margin required:** 5%

59 It is worth noting that, in certain markets, the rights obtained by a securities lender with regards to collateral may be less than full ownership.
60 Most securities lending facilities are open so that lenders have the right to recall specific securities, but most lenders seek to minimise these recalls. There were, however, significant recalls during the Asian financial crises in the 1990s of securities supporting short positions as lenders scrambled to trade out their positions, resulting in some squeezes in the market.

- **Collateral required:** value of the equities borrowed + 5% margin = £525,000.00 in UK gilts
- **Daily lending income for lender:** loan value * (number of days borrowed/365) * lending fee
  = 500,000 * (1/365) * 0.005 = £6.85

In the event of the loan being outstanding for a month and paid back on the 20 July 2008, the custody bank receives two streams of income:

On 30 June 2008 lending fees = £6.85 * 10 days = £68.50
On 31 July 2008 lending fees = £6.85 * 20 days = £137.00

Therefore total revenue is £205.50, against which the cost of settling the transaction (loan and collateral) must be offset.

It is important to note that the example assumes that the value of the security on the loan has remained constant in order to ensure clarity. But in reality, the price would change daily when the value is marked to market, different fees would be chargeable per day and changes in the value of the collateral would be required. In addition, as the term of the loan is open, the transaction can only be re-rated or have the fees amended if market circumstances change. This is also part of the assumption in this illustration.

Figure 8.3 depicts a scenario whereby collateral is being held by a tri-party agent. In this case, a specialist agent such as an International Central Securities Depository will receive only eligible collateral to market, with information distributed to both lender and borrower (see dotted "Reporting" lines). Normally the tri-party agent charges the borrower a fee.

Figure 8.3 Collateralised Transaction with Collateral held by Tri-party Agent

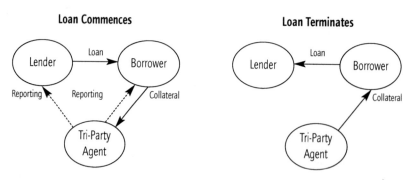

Source: An Introduction to Securities Lending © Mark C. Faulkner

Transaction collateralised with cash

Cash collateral is popular in the USA and Europe and is an integral part of a prime broker's securities lending activities. Generally, when cash is received by the lender as collateral, it is reinvested into short-term money market instruments. In return, the lender pays the prime broker a rate of interest on the cash collateral called the "rebate" rate. The lender then earns the spread between the investment rate of the short-term vehicle and the rebate rate.

Figure 8.4 Collateralised Transaction with Cash as Collateral

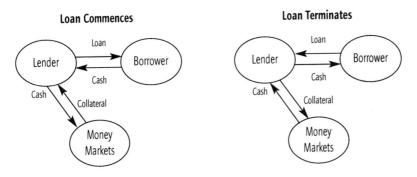

Source: An Introduction to Securities Lending © Mark C. Faulkner

Example 2: The following is an illustration of a securities loan collateralised with cash.
Transaction date: 19 June 2008
Settlement date: 20 June 2008
Term: Open
Security: BizCorp
Security price: £10.00 per share
Quantity: 50,000 shares
Loan value: £500,000.00
Rebate rate: 80 basis points
Collateral: USD cash
Margin required: 5%
Collateral required: $1,034,250.00 (£525,000.00 * 1.97)
Reinvestment rate: 130 basis points
Daily lending income: $14.36 or £7.29 ($1,034,250 * 0.005 * (1/360))

FX rate used for computation is £1.00 = $1.97

In similar circumstances to Example 1, if this transaction remains outstanding for one month and is returned on the 20 July 2008, there will be two cash flow streams from the lender to the prime broker based upon the cash collateral, and the lender makes a profit from the 50 basis points spread between the reinvestment rate and the rebate rate.

$1,034,250.00 * 0.008*(1/360) = $22.98

Payments to the prime broker:
On 30 June 2008 = $22.98 * 10 days = $229.80

On 31 July 2008 = $22.98 * 20 days = $459.67

The lender's profit will typically be calculated thus:
On 30 June 2008 = £7.29 * 10 days = £72.90
On 31 July 2008 = £7.29 * 20 days = £145.80

The total revenue to the lender is £218.70. The cost of settling the transactions (loan and collateral) is offset against this value.

Repurchase agreements

A repurchase agreement (or repo) is a securities lending transaction between two parties whereby one party agrees to sell the other a security against a transfer of cash at a specified price, with a commitment to buy the security back at a later date for another specified price. In this type of securities lending transaction, the prime broker that is borrowing securities is referred to as the buyer, while the lender is referred to as the seller. Most repos are governed by a master agreement known as the TBMA/ISMA Global Master Repurchase Agreement (GMRA).

Repo transactions are executed for two major reasons:

1. To transfer ownership of a particular security between parties;
2. Facilitation of collateralised cash loans or funding transactions.

Repos are similar to securities loans that are collateralised against cash, given the interest rate element in the income that is implicit in the pricing of the two legs of the transaction.

At the onset of the transaction, securities are valued and sold at the prevailing market price plus any coupon that has accrued, i.e. the dirty price. At termination, the securities are resold at a predetermined price equal to the original price plus interest at a previously agreed rate (the repo rate).

In securities-driven transactions (i.e. where the motivation extends beyond simply financing), the repo rate is normally set at a lower rate than current money market rates to compensate the lender who will invest the funds in the money markets and will want a return. The lender often receives a margin by pricing the securities above the market level.

In cash-driven transactions, the repurchase price will usually be agreed at a level close to current money market yields, given that this is a financing as opposed to a security-specific transaction. The right to substitute "repoed" securities as collateral is agreed by the parties at the beginning of the repo transaction. A margin is usually provided to the lender of cash by discounting the value of the transferred securities by an agreed "haircut".

The following is an illustration of a repo transaction.

BizFund, a fictional hedge fund, requires cash for 30 days from 9 March to 8 April and provides EUR 100 million German Bund (4.25% 26 January 2017) as collateral, quoting a repo rate of 1.56%.

Figure 8.5 Repurchase Agreement

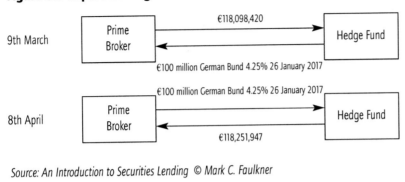

Source: An Introduction to Securities Lending © Mark C. Faulkner

The following is the calculation of the amount of cash provided by the prime brokers and the repo interest paid by the hedge fund.

Current market price	115.12373
3% haircut	(3.45371)
Accrued interest as of 9 February	6.42840
All-in-price	118.09842

Amount of cash
provided by prime broker = nominal value of collateral * (all-in price/100)
= 100,000,000*(118.09842/100) = EUR 118,098,420

Repo interest to be paid
to prime broker = EUR 118,098,420 * (30/360) days) * 1.56% = EUR 153,527.95

Buy/ sell backs and sell/ buy backs

Buy/sell backs are similar in economic terms to repos but differ in the way they are structured. Buy/sell backs are structured as a sale and simultaneous purchase of securities, with the purchase agreed for a future settlement date. The price of the forward purchase is usually calculated and agreed by referring to the market repo rate. A buy/sell back is the equivalent of a reverse repo. However, there are differences between the two structures in that while a repo is, in theory, a single transaction, a buy/sell is a pair of transactions, i.e. a sell and a buy.

In buy/sell back transactions, the purchaser of the securities receives absolute title to them and holds on to any accrued interest and coupon payments over the course of the transaction. However, the coupons received by the purchaser are factored into the price of the forward contract.

A sell/buy back is the equivalent of a classic repo.
The following transaction illustrates a sell/buy back transaction.

A hedge fund intends to borrow JPY 100 million JGB (6.00% 7 December 2037) from 14 September to 13 October. A prime broker quotes a rate of 5.63%.
The calculation of repo interest to be paid to the prime broker is as follows.

Figure 8.6 Sell–buy back transaction

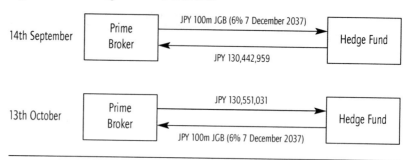

The buy transaction for 14 September is priced as follows:

Current market price   128.82000
Accrued interest as of 14 September   1.62295
All-in price   130.44295
Cash provided by hedge fund = nominal amount * (all-in price)
                = 100,000,000 * (130.44295) = JPY 130,442,950

Repo interest to be paid to prime broker using the act/365 day count convention:
JPY 130,442,950 * (29/365 days) * 5.63% = JPY 583,491

Pricing the sellback transaction for 13 October:
All-in buy price   130.44295
Repo interest   0.583491
Accrued interest as of 13 October   (0.475410)
Sellback price quoted   130.551031

Therefore, the hedge fund sells back JPY 100 million JGB at the prearranged price of JPY 130,551,031.

Revenue generation from securities lending

Revenue can be affected by many factors. These include:

- availability of security in open market;
- value of portfolio;
- asset class;
- duration of loan;
- size of individual holdings;
- type of investment strategy;
- market/geographic diversification;
- dividend yield of security;
- tax status of underlying lender.

Risks

As securities lending transactions take place in existing securities clearance and settlement systems, the types and sources of risk are consequently of the same kind as those faced by prime brokers in outright securities transactions. Financial risks in securities lending are mostly managed through the use of collateral and netting. As stated earlier, collateral can be in the form of cash or securities.

Prime brokers that are counterparties in securities lending transactions are aware of the heightened and extended duration of their exposure to these risks. Given that there are two legs in the transaction, the risks for counterparties span the entire life cycle from execution of the trade through to settlement of the return of borrowed securities or cash.

Types and Sources of Risk

Credit risk

This is the risk from uncertainty in the counterparty's ability to settle an obligation for full value when it is due. This could apply to the failure to settle the obligation at any time thereafter. Prime brokers are focused on the mitigation of two types of credit risk: principal risk and replacement cost risk. These types of risk are described as follows:

- **Principal risk** – This is perceived as the largest credit risk that either counterparty in a trade is exposed to. It is the loss of the full value of securities or funds that a non-defaulting counterparty has shifted to the defaulting counterparty. The exposure of a non-defaulting counterparty to principal risk is exemplified by the following instances:
    - uncollateralisation of securities lending transactions;
    - the failure to complete the settlement of either the first or second leg of the transaction as expected, i.e. settlement risk.

    It is worth noting that the lender is at risk at the settlement of the initial loan and the borrower is at risk at the return leg if completion of the delivery of collateral of securities of funds is possible without receiving the delivery of collateral.

- **Replacement cost risk** – A settlement failure exposes a lender and borrower to replacement cost risk. This type of risk can arise in securities lending transactions even where transactions are fully collateralised and where a DVP (or DVD) settlement mechanism is employed. If a situation arises whereby a securities lending counterparty defaults while the loan is outstanding, the non-defaulting counterparty would usually look to effect a "buy-in". For a lender, this involves liquidating any collateral and buying the loaned securities in the open market. As a consequence, the non-defaulting counterparty may be exposed to the risk that will incur a cost (a loss) in replacing the contract. Such a loss will occur for a lender only if, at the time of the default, the loaned asset has a positive market value relative to the

Figure 8.7 Comparisons of Securities Lending, Repo and Buy/ Sell Back

Characteristic	Securities Lending		Repo		Buy/ Sell Back
	Cash collateral	Securities/ other non-cash collateral	Specific securities (securities-driven)	General Collateral (cash-driven)	
Formal method of exchange	Sale with agreement to make subsequent reacquisition of equivalent securities	Sale with agreement to make subsequent reacquisition of equivalent securities	Sale and repurchase under terms of master agreement	Sale and repurchase under terms of master agreement	Sale and repurchase
Form of exchange	Securities vs cash	Securities vs collateral (NB. often free of payment but sometimes delivery vs delivery)	Securities vs cash (NB. often delivery vs payment)	Cash vs securities (NB. often delivery vs payment)	Cash vs securities (NB. often delivery vs payment)
Collateral type	Cash	Securities (bonds and equities), letters of credit, DBVs, CDs	Cash	General collateral (bonds) or acceptable collateral as defined by buyer)	Typically bonds
Return is paid to the supplier of	Cash collateral	Loan securities (not collateral securities	Cash	Cash	Cash
Return payable as	Rebate interest (ie. return paid on cash lower than comparable cash market interest rates)	Fee, e.g. standard fees for FTSE 100 stocks are about 6–8 basis points (ie. 0.06–0.08% pa)	Quoted as repo rate, paid as interest on the cash collateral (lower than general collatoral repo rate)	Quoted as repo rate, paid as interest on the cash	Quoted as repo rate, paid through the price differential between sale price and repurchase price

Initial margin	Yes	Yes	Yes	Yes	Possible
Variation margin	Yes	Yes	Yes	Yes	No (only possible through close out and repricing)
Over-collateralisation	Yes (in favour of the securities lender)	Yes (in favour of the securities lender)	No	Possible (if any, in favour of the cash provider)	Possible (if any, in favour of the cash provider)
Collateral substitution	Yes (determined by borrower)	Yes (determined by borrower)	No	Yes (determined by the original seller)	No (only possible through close out and repricing)
Dividends and coupons	Manufactured to the lender	Manufactured to the lender	Paid to the original seller	Paid to the original seller	No formal obligation to return income normally factored into the buy-back price
Legal set off in event of default	Yes	Yes	Yes	Yes	No
Maturity	Open or term	Open or term	Open or term	Open or term	Term only
Typical asset type	Bonds and equities	Bonds and equities	Mainly bonds, equities possible	Mainly bonds, equities possible	Almost entirely bonds
Motivation	Security specific dominant	Security specific	Security specific	Financing	Financing dominant
Payment	Monthly in arrears	Monthly in arrears	At maturity	At maturity	At maturity

Source: An Introduction to Securities Lending © *Mark C. Faulkner*

collateral value. On the other hand, the party borrowing securities and funds would normally have the right to the return of collateral from a defaulting counterparty and would only be exposed to a replacement cost risk if the collateral instrument had a positive market value relative to the borrowed asset. An assessment of replacement cost risk must entail an assessment of:

- the probability of the counterparty defaulting;
- the credit exposure (the potential magnitude of the positive market value, if any) at the time of default.

Liquidity risk

This is the risk associated with the failure of a counterparty to settle an obligation for full value when due, but can effect settlement on an unspecified later date. The reason for the failure to settle may be temporary, such as the inability to meets its obligations when due as a result of a demand for securities or funds that is too large. In this case, the event will be termed a failed transaction rather than a default. Another example may be where investors holding short positions cannot obtain the securities needed to unwind the securities borrowing.

Market risk

This is the risk of loss from unfavourable movements in the volatility of the market prices of assets. Analysis of market risk can only be meaningfully achieved on a portfolio basis, allowing for offsetting positions in particular underlying risk factors such as interest rates, exchange rates, commodities prices or equity indices and correlations among those risk factors. In securities lending transactions, market risk can occur in such cases as:

- inappropriate margining;
- reinvestment of cash collateral;
- a counterparty default.

Settlement risk

This is the risk that settlement of individual transactions will not occur as expected. Two principal sources of settlement risk are:

- a time-lag between the completion of two legs of the transaction, i.e. any lag between payment leg and delivery leg;
- a time-lag between the execution of the transaction and its final completion.

Before discussing the controls that prime brokers put in place to mitigate risk, it is essential to discuss the reasons for settlement fails.

Settlement Fails[61]

Settlement fails usually occur when securities are not delivered and not paid for on the date originally scheduled by borrower and lender in the securities lending transaction. Fails occur for a variety of reasons. One major reason is miscommunication. Regardless of their best efforts to agree on terms, a borrower and lender may sometimes not communicate in the same way for a given transaction to their respective operations departments. On the settlement date, the lender may deliver what it believes is the correct quantity of the correct security and claim what it believes is the correct payment, but the borrower will reject the delivery if it has a different understanding of the transaction. If the rejection occurs late in the day, there may not be enough time for the counterparties to resolve the misunderstanding.

In some instances a lender may be unable to deliver securities because of operational problems. An extreme example is the 11 September 2001 catastrophe that destroyed banking offices and records, impaired telecommunications links between market participants, and damaged other essential infrastructure.

Fails also occur when special collateral repo rates approach or reach zero. Generally, a market participant would be better off borrowing securities to avoid a fail even if the interest on the money lent in the special market is below the general collateral repo rate because the alternative is forgoing interest altogether. However, this incentive becomes less compelling as a special rate approaches zero. A special rate will approach zero if there is unusually strong demand to borrow security, for example following heavy short selling by hedgers, or if holders are unusually reluctant to lend the security.

Risk Controls

Prime brokers need to put controls in place to manage the risks described above. Figure 8.8 lists some types of risks and the associated controls. These controls can ensure that risk can be mitigated to such an extent that it can be reduced to very low levels. Risk reduction is increasingly important as securities lending is a huge factor in world financial markets as well as an important source of liquidity.

---

61   This section draws upon the paper of Michael J. Fleming and Kenneth D. Garbade, "When the Back Office Moved to the Front Burner: Settlement Fails in the Treasury Market after 9/11", Federal Reserve Bank of New York Economic Policy Review, November 2002.

Figure 8.8 Risk Controls

Risk	Controls
Counterparty risk Borrower defaults or is insolvent, failing to re-deliver the borrowed securities	• Capital and rating requirements, extensive ongoing credit reviews and VaR-based credit limits. • Daily collateral mark-to-market • Indemnification insurance provided by third party in the event of borrower default
Cash collateral reinvestment risk Investment default, credit risk and liquidity or duration mismatch in the cash reinvestment portfolio	• Monitor and manage average-weighted life, credit quality, sector allocation, duration and liquidity • Establish conservative reinvestment guidelines • Manage unbundling of "core" cash management
Operational risk Processing mistakes and errors in administering lending programs	• Daily reconciliation between program participants • Process and procedures in a controlled environment • Routine reporting and compliance monitoring
Legal/contractual risk Compliance with program guidelines	• Standardised documentation • Audit/compliance reporting and oversight • Premier industry experts as external legal counsel

Source: eSecLending

Common Systems Used in Prime Brokerage

9

This chapter contains information about common systems used in prime brokerage.

Introduction

Technology is one area of the prime brokerage business that is lowering the barriers to entry and has been partly responsible for the breakdown of the oligopoly that once existed in this sector of the financial services industry.

In the highly competitive prime brokerage marketplace, the goal of each prime broker is to offer services at the lowest possible cost, bring as many new clients online as rapidly as possible, and be able to react quickly to market dynamics and market threats as well as client requirements.

In order to achieve these objectives, prime brokers seek to create an enhanced IT infrastructure and the capabilities to configure and automate the real-time interchange of data, in various message formats, across organisational boundaries.

Hedge fund managers are usually very familiar with the technology requirements of their businesses and, given the increasing competition in the marketplace, there has to be an advance in the level of technology provided if a prime broker wants to remain competitive. Furthermore, in recent times, systems and connectivity have become an issue of coverage and seamless integration. In order for a prime broker to offer full-prime prime brokerage services, it needs to offer service offerings to its clients in each of the key technology areas demanded by hedge funds. These areas include order management systems (OMS), execution management systems (EMS) and direct market access (DMA) integration, research and pre-trade tools as well as portfolio analysis and risk management tools. Prime brokers are seeking to make each of these technology tools available as options to clients to enable them to make a choice and integrate them into their own environment with as little effort as possible.

Hedge fund clients trading anonymously through DMA platforms, however, pose a challenge to prime brokers. Lately, hedge funds have been increasingly renting the prime broker's infrastructure to get the best execution across multiple venues as opposed to traditional practice whereby a hedge fund manager telephoned the sell-side trader at, say, an investment bank, to issue verbal instructions. The safety checks in the conventional model are not available when trading via DMA platforms.

Industry experts, however, believe that DMA trading by hedge fund clients increases the risks incurred by prime brokers because these clients can place orders faster that they can monitor the risk. In addition, if a hedge fund client utilises multiple executing dealers that give access to their own DMA platforms, then the prime broker may not be aware of all of the orders before close of trading, meaning that they cannot calculate margin deposits in real time. Furthermore, these so-called margin engines are not updated until the prime broker receives entire information on the hedge fund's position at the end of the day.

There is inherent risk in a typical scenario whereby a hedge fund is trading with one executing dealer and giving it up to another prime broker as one of the parties has to bear the risk from the time the trade is taken up and accepted by the prime broker. This situation becomes increasingly complex as hedge funds expand their trading across multiple asset classes.

The systems used in the prime brokerage industry are increasingly being developed to enable their hedge fund clients to utilise multiple prime brokers. Traditionally, most hedge funds have relied broadly on prime brokers to provide and run the middle- and back-office software they need. In most cases, however, this middle- and back-office software can accommodate only one prime broker, thus hedge funds using multiple prime brokers have encountered some difficult problems.

A common problem has been the need to collect data from several prime brokers with software that could accommodate only a single prime broker. As a result, the data transfer process could be a major source of error. Another was that prime brokers were compelled to share the details of their hedge fund clients with other prime brokers who were their competitors. This put these hedge fund clients in an awkward position as they were not comfortable with letting any prime broker know what they were doing with other prime brokers.

Vendors, alerted to this situation, have been developing suites of software products that aggregate data for hedge funds from multiple prime brokers, maintain the confidentiality that hedge funds want, and perform all of the various different and complex tracking, accounting and reporting functions that hedge funds need to do.

The Prime Brokerage Technology Market

The prime brokerage technology market is set for rapid growth, given the rapid increase in technology development within the prime brokerage universe. The decision to build or buy technology is shaping the technology market in the industry. While there are plenty of packaged solutions that support the trading life cycle which prime brokers can buy, they need to customise their applications for their increasingly sophisticated hedge fund clients. Industry experts also assert that prime brokers need a flexible IT set-up that allows them to exploit non-traditional revenue-earning asset classes such as derivatives. All these factors are drivers for growth in the prime brokerage technology market.

Hedge fund needs in terms of electronic execution is another driver for growth. A 2008 FINalternatives Prime Brokerage Survey showed that of the respondents, a large proportion, 30%, characterise their electronic platform needs as "advanced", while another 60% characterise those needs as "middle-of-the-road". This implies that demand for electronic trading systems will be on the rise in the prime brokerage industry.

Furthermore, industry reports show that prime brokers will continue to invest in pricing analytics and algorithmic trading tools in order to continue to achieve best execution for their hedge fund clients. In addition, risk analytics and monitoring, compliance, and portfolio valuation are among the determinants of IT spending in the industry.

It is expected that the growth in IT spending will be in double digits by 2015.

Profile of systems

The following are profiles of two of the leading vendors in the prime brokerage space.

Paladyne Suite of Products

Paladyne Systems provide a technology platform for global hedge funds and prime brokers. The Paladyne suite of products integrates the front-, middle- and back-office, focusing on order management/execution management, global reference data administration and comprehensive reporting tools. Paladyne integrates and supports a full complement of partnerships required by hedge funds to offer a "one-stop solution" that includes accounting systems, data providers and execution management systems.

The Paladyne difference

According to Paladyne, *"As the alternative investment space becomes more complex, hedge funds and prime brokers are looking for a scalable solution that will seamlessly connect the front-, middle- and back-office functions while controlling operational and technology costs. Additionally, depending on business requirements, any components of the PALADYNE suite can be integrated as "stand-alone" in a fully hosted or local install."*

The Paladyne product suite

The PALADYNE™ suite was developed by a large multi-strategy hedge fund as a solution to the challenging business requirements facing a global investment company. The design concept is based on the centralisation of common business processes such as security master maintenance, pricing, trade capture and allocation, data warehousing, and reporting. By using a centralised middleware platform, hedge funds can add or change internal systems such as execution platforms, risk engines and modelling applications without changing their core infrastructure. The PALADYNE suite includes a flexible adaptor layer and a comprehensive posting and distribution engine for integrating and synchronising data amongst internal and external systems.

Paladyne offers a complete suite of products to efficiently handle trade execution and straight-through processing, global "golden copy" reference data management, flexible presentation, reporting and full general ledger accounting. The managed and hosted PALADYNE suite includes:

■ **Paladyne Portfolio Master**™: provides multi-asset class order management (OMS), customisable allocation tools, fund modelling, and real-time fund P&L tracking.
■ **Paladyne Analytics Master**™: provides integrated cross-data aggregation and warehousing, on-line data analysis, reconciliation and data exchange hub, and reporting tools for centralised firm-wide data mining and custom reporting.

- **Paladyne Security Master™**: is a security-level reference data management tool that provides a centralised terms and conditions repository, distribution engine to manage upstream and downstream security requests, full OTC support, real-time corporate action alerts and daily event tracking.
- **Paladyne Price Master™**: is a pricing-level reference data management tool that provides automated collection, storage and analysis of prices and market data, customisable pricing rules, and comprehensive audit and compliance reporting.
- **Advent Geneva®**: Paladyne offers Advent Geneva® as one of the back-office portfolio accounting modules available as part of Paladyne's hosted solution. Paladyne is the only provider of an ASP-based version of Advent Geneva and has fully integrated Advent Geneva with each of the PALADYNE suite products. Advent Geneva coupled with Paladyne's front- and middle-office product suite provides a world-class technology platform for hedge funds and hedge fund services providers.
- **Sungard Visual Portfolio Manager™ (VPM)**: Sungard VPM offers a comprehensive, multi-currency, fully integrated and customisable investment management solution. Paladyne offers and integrates Sungard VPM as one of the back-office accounting modules available in the Paladyne hosted solution.
- **Data Vendors**: Paladyne offers a multitude of choices for its clients and partners for real-time data, securities terms and conditions, corporate actions, and end-of-day prices. Paladyne's partners include: Bloomberg, Thomson Reuters, IDC, S&P, and Markit Partners.
- **NumeriX™**: Paladyne offers NumeriX models for pricing complex derivatives in both real time and as part of the end-of-day valuation process. Integrated with Paladyne Portfolio Master and Paladyne Price Master, NumeriX provides an addition to the PALADYNE suite to service both the front- and back-office needs.

Selective clients include prime brokers such as Credit Suisse.

SunGard

SunGard is a provider of software and processing solutions to financial services companies in more than 50 countries. The SunGard suite of products for the securities finance industry provides a complete solution for trade entry/maintenance, consolidated position and inventory management, cash and non-cash collateral management, delivery/settlement interfaces, risk management and other trade life-cycle processing activities as well as reporting. Market data analytics and analysis of stock loan performance are also incorporated within the product offerings.

Global One, Martini, Loanet and Astec combine to form the SunGard solution that prime brokers use to support the full range of securities lending and repo activities. All products can be fully integrated into a client's upstream and downstream systems (for example global credit and risk systems) to facilitate efficiency of front-to-back operation.

Global One

Global One is a comprehensive mid-to-back office solution for international securities lending, supporting both lenders and borrowers. It provides prime brokers with a real-time solution for the accounting, reporting and management of their securities lending activities.

Key features

- Links with trading and order-routing systems to maximise automated trading.
- Support for both principal and agency trading.
- Standard "out of the box" settlement links with standard settlement systems.
- Collateral management for cash and non-cash collateral.
- Credit limit processing to minimise securities finance-specific operational risk.
- Entitlements processing to highlight actions and to manage the impact on underlying trades.
- Generation of detailed (and summary) fee statement, plus management of fee collection cycle.
- Comprehensive trade life-cycle activity audit.

Martini

Martini is a front- and middle-office securities finance solution for international equity and fixed income products. It provides a global real-time trading platform for prime brokers in stock loans and repos.

Martini also facilitates multi-entity and multi-currency trading, with a user-defined book structure and flexible trading views to allow users to maximise the potential of their tradable assets.

Prime brokers use Martini for:

- real-time global positions management;
- flexible entity and book structures;
- legal agreement tracking and controls;
- tailored and streamlined trade capture;
- collateral optimisation and management (cash and non-cash);
- risk management;
- mid-office trade support activities;
- profit and loss reporting.

Loanet

Loanet is used by US prime brokers and is an integrated accounting service for US domestic securities lending. The full service provides a specialised subsidiary ledger for all securities lending accounting and operations, incorporating comprehensive interfaces with Depository Trust & Clearing Corporation (DTCC) and the Canadian Depository System (CDS). The select services offer the benefits of automation of firm-to-firm trade life-cycle activities such as comparison, marks and recalls within the linked community of securities lending market participants, covering the majority of the US domestic market.

Key features

- Full trade life-cycle management, incorporating specialised accounting subledger.
- Securities finance hub linking over 200 borrowers and lenders.
- Order routing to automate the borrowing and lending of securities.
- Settlement links to DTCC and CDS to handle all stock loan-related activities.
- Contract and rebate compare to eliminate errors before they become costly and time-consuming to correct.
- Loanet Automated Marks (LAMS) to automate daily mark-to-market.
- Automated Recalls (ARMS) and Automated Returns (LARS) to automate recalls and intra-day loan returns.
- Risk management is provided with credit limits, concentration limits, mark-to-market reports and a variety of DTCC balancing tools.
- Efficient, single point of delivery for distribution of Agency Lending Disclosure information between lenders and borrowers.

Astec Analytics

The Astec Analytics suite of products is used by prime brokers for discovery of price and market information, to support the trader in accurate stock loan pricing. It is also used to provide a series of performance benchmarking and board reporting services.

Key features

- Lending Pit trading information tool for up-to-date loan rates and market colour.
- Data feed of daily market information.
- Peer group benchmarking, portfolio evaluation and relationship-based reporting for hedge fund clients.
- Performance analytics for desk managers.
- Tracking of the market for potential events.
- Custom analysis and reporting.
- "State of the market" reporting.

List of other systems

System	Vendor / Provider	Uses
Trade Suite/ CNS Interface	National Securities Clearing Corporation (NSCC)	It is used to streamline trade processing and reduce risk to both the prime broker and the executing broker
TRM-Prime Broker (TRM-PB)	Traiana	Used for managing the entire post-trade, pre-booking process in prime brokerage
Beauchamp	Linedata	Used to provide clients with a platform to manage complex portfolios as well as satisfy investor and regulatory requirements
T Zero Prime Brokerage	T Zero	Used by prime brokers to automate the "give-up" process
Geneva	Advent	Used for client portfolio accounting including general ledger reporting, performance measurement and portfolio reporting
Swaps Pricing Platform	SQX	Used for accessing security quotes generated by broker-dealers that prime brokers use for calculating clients' net asset values (NAVs)
TradeTracker Prime	MezzoWare	Used to enable clients to report their trades that prime brokers should be informed of
Prime Brokerage Online Reporting	Actuate	Used to provide performance, balance and trade confirmations for clients
Derivatives.com	Imagine Trading	An application service provided to prime brokers to allow their clients access to risk management and trading services
TradeSmart	TradingScreen	Used to provide clients with a platform to trade a variety of financial instruments
Advisorware	SS&C	Portfolio management, accounting and partnership accounting used by hedge fund clients, which prime brokers can access to view the portfolio of the client
Prime brokerage for matching on Reuters	Thomson Reuters	Used to allow clients to trade on Reuters, matching in the name of and utilising the credit of the prime broker
TradeXpress	Thomson	Used to allocate and confirm fixed income trades

PBWire	Markit	Trade acceptance service for OTC interest rate derivatives trade intermediation as well as trade notification and confirmation
Scrittura	Interwoven Inc.	Automation and validation of trade confirmations and supporting documents for OTC derivative instruments
Compliance Hub	Communicator Inc	Post-trade automation, exception handling for derivative products such as credit and equity swaps
Financial Calendar	Swaps Monitor Publications Inc.	Global database of holidays used to reduce the number of expensive date discrepancies that arise during the trade confirmation process
Visual Portfolio Manager (VPM)	Integrated Business Systems Incorporated (now a part of Sungard)	Portfolio accounting, trade processing and reporting system used by hedge fund clients, which prime brokers can access to view the portfolio of the client

IT Projects

This chapter contains discussions of the implementation of the multi-prime brokerage environment, IT security and of Green IT strategies that are the basis for IT projects in prime brokerage.

Introduction

Prime brokerage is an important aspect of doing business with hedge funds. As a result, IT projects that are undertaken within the prime brokerage function of investment banks have to reflect this importance. These projects cut across the different service offerings of prime brokers and are essential to the smooth delivery of these services to hedge funds.

Effective project management is required for IT projects in prime brokerage, given that hedge fund clients rely on prime brokers for support of their range of activities from trade execution to clearing and settlement. These projects are managed according to the tenets of the project management discipline, ensuring that they are delivered on time and within budget.

One differentiating aspect of IT projects in prime brokerage that sets them apart from most other projects in investment banks is the need to deliver on requirements driven by the needs of the external clients. Therefore, it is essential that they are managed in an efficient manner and their success safeguards the reputations of both the prime broker and their parent investment bank.

In an age when hedge funds are becoming increasingly regulated, technological support provided by prime brokers is invaluable in aiding hedge funds, especially the start-ups that are heavily reliant on prime brokers, to comply with current and future regulations. Hence, it is essential that hedge funds have a holistic view of their trading positions as well as accounting data. Successful IT projects involving implementation and support of relevant IT systems can make this happen.

Types of IT Projects

The following are IT projects that can be undertaken by prime brokers to improve their operational efficiencies.

Implementing a Multi-Prime Brokerage Environment[62]
When a hedge fund chooses to introduce additional prime brokers into its operating environment, it is essential that the managers are aware of the challenges involved. The level of complexity is directly linked to the extent to which the hedge fund relies on the initial prime broker for tools, such as intra-day P&L, position and risk reporting, investors reporting, etc. The more systems that are either maintained in-house or by a neutral third-party provider, the less complicated it is to add a prime broker.

---

62 This section draws on the June 2008 paper "The Multi-Prime Broker Environment: Overcoming the Challenges and Reaping the Benefits" by Merrill Lynch Global Markets Financing & Services.

Data Aggregation

Hedge fund managers need to make some key decisions when making the transition to a multi-prime brokerage environment. One of key decisions is the process for daily data aggregation. A prime broker has visibility to the entire hedge fund's book if it is the only prime broker the hedge fund utilises. It is easy for the sole prime broker to provide position, cash balance and risk reports for the entire portfolio, given that all the trade and position data are maintained in one place. As soon as additional prime brokers are introduced, it is then imperative to aggregate data from multiple primes in order to generate consolidated reports, including whole portfolio risk, portfolio accounting and performance metrics. Three options for data aggregation for a fund utilising a number of prime brokers are as follows:

1. deciding on an allocation methodology for attributing trades to each prime broker;
2. aggregation of trade and position data from multiple prime brokers to generate consolidated reports: risk, portfolio, accounting and performance;
3. signing of new documentation, reflecting:
   - changes in signing authority;
   - changes in regulatory authority;
   - ISDA agreements with credit terms appropriate to the fund;
   - corporate or management changes since inception.

Hearsay reporting capabilities of the first prime broker

This can be described as the "first step" in the process of creating a multi-prime environment. In some situations, the prime broker with the majority of the hedge fund assets (typically the initial prime broker) will request a feed of trades and positions from the second prime broker and aggregate them into their customary reports and statements. It can be argued that this is perhaps the easiest and least disruptive option for the hedge fund because the manager will carry on receiving the same consolidated reports from the initial prime broker that they are used to.

It is important to note that using hearsay reports cancels out one of the major benefits of using multi-prime brokers, i.e. risk diversification and prevention of any one prime broker from having complete knowledge of the fund's portfolio. In addition, the dependence on hearsay reporting is not typically a scalable solution. When a hedge fund adds more prime brokers, more balances are shifted away from the initial prime broker which could potentially reduce the prime broker's willingness to offer hearsay reporting.

Utilising a fund administrator

As fund administrators' primary function from an operational standpoint is to consolidate a hedge fund's data from multiple sources with a view to independently valuing the fund's entire portfolio, they can generate consolidated versions of the common report that prime brokers produce (risk, position, cash balance etc.). As far as data aggregation problems are concerned, the use of fund administration as a solution is more scalable that hearsay reporting. There are other advantages of using fund administrators as each prime broker can only view their section of the hedge fund's portfolio.

Building in-house capabilities

This solution, while generally more flexible and costly, entails implementing internal systems that will consolidate the data across all prime brokers and generate all the necessary reports internally. At the outset, these types of implementation involve the use of a vendor-supplied order management system to control allocation of trades across multiple prime brokers (see Figure 10.1). Third-party accounting solutions can be used to fulfil the requirements for control over in-house data aggregation requirements, internal and investor reporting requirements, and accounting. These systems will need to be customised and integrated with prevailing applications and data existing within the fund. Self-sufficiency and total control over the fund's data is a significant benefit to be derived from this approach, in spite of the considerable cost, both in terms of the vendor software and the IT services/personnel needed to implement and maintain these systems. This is an important aspect of hedge fund operations, especially for those operating in the multi-asset class domain, given their misgivings about their inability to access their data from external vendors and service providers. Hedge funds that opt for in-house solutions may do away with outside providers for their custom reporting, data extracts and so on. In addition, each prime broker will continue to have access to only their section of the portfolio.

The data aggregation options discussed thus far obviously differ in operational complexity as well as costs. Nevertheless, an analytical process is required to decide on the most appropriate method. This process starts with the identification of the key reports that are utilised by the hedge fund in the single prime broker environment. The next step involves the individual analysis of each report with a view to determining the optimum way it can be generated.

The flowchart in Figure 10.2 is a diagrammatic representation of the analytical process that can be relevant to each key report.

Trade Allocation and Position Maintenance

As well as the analysis of data aggregation measures, there is the need to determine a trade allocation methodology. As seen in previous chapters, hedge fund trades are allocated to their prime broker, but in a multi-prime broker environment, a trading allocation methodology that specifies to which prime broker a given trade will be allocated is required. Typical examples of trade allocation methodologies include:

- specifying a single prime broker for each legal entity;
- specifying a single prime broker for each strategy;
- utilising a pre-defined ratio to split allocations across prime brokers, a typical example being the splitting of each trade evenly between two prime brokers.

Figure 10.1 Options for Data Aggregation

Options	Pros	Cons
Hearsay by Prime Broker with bulk of assets	• Easiest implementation • Least expensive option • Already familiar with report formats	• Not scalable – hard to add a third or fourth Prime Broker • "Prime" Prime Broker can still view entire portfolio • Dependency on "Prime" Prime Broker's release schedule, willingness to accommodate hearsay, etc.
Fund administrator	• Scalable up to any number of Prime Brokers • Each Prime Broker only views its portion of the portolio • Usually more cost-effective than doing all aggregation and reporting in-house	• Additional expense *(to the fund)* • Some have difficulty with exotic products • Must get familiar with new report formats
Build in-house capabilities	• Most flexible • Each Prime Broker only views its portion of the portfolio • All data remains in-house	• Most costly in both time and expense *(usually borne by the management company)*

Source: Merrill Lynch Global Markets Financing and Markets

Methodologies for allocating trades to multiple prime brokers

Figure 10.3 shows methodologies for allocating trades to multiple prime brokers.

Industry experts assert that it is necessary to factor in the impact of cross-margining when choosing a trade allocation process. In a situation whereby a hedge fund is trading off-setting positions that can potentially reduce collateral requirements at a prime broker, it is essential that the offsetting trades are allocated to the same prime broker.

Case Study

The case study below briefly describes the benefits of implementing a multi-prime brokerage system using Paladyne as an example.

Background

A leading multi-strategy hedge fund manager with more than $2 billion under management had quadrupled its assets in three years.

Business Knowledge for IT in Prime Brokerage

Figure 10.2 Analysis Process for Report Generation

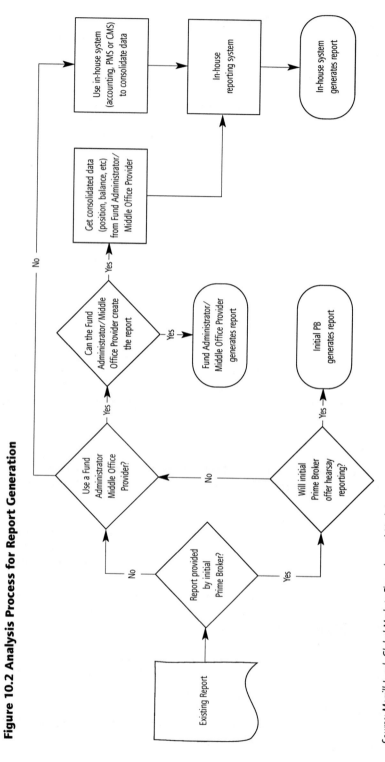

Source: Merrill Lynch Global Markets Financing and Markets

Figure 10.3 Trade allocation methodologies

Simple/ Static	• By Fund • By Market • By Strategy	Easiest to implement, but can be difficult to adjust in order to maintain target asset levels with each Prime Broker
Granular/ Dynamic	• By Security • On a pro rata basis • Arbitrary method	More complex to implement, but can be recalibrated when target allocations of balances across prime brokers are reviewed and changed
Opportunistic	• By borrow availability • By executing Broker	Used in conjunction with one of the others as a "fine-tuning" method to optimise financing benefits

Source: Merrill Lynch Global Markets Financing and Markets

Due to the fast growth, spreadsheets emerged as the de facto solution of choice for all information demands. The front office was looking for various tools with no success and the back office was stretched to support the firm's growth. The firm had multiple information technology systems and many spreadsheets containing duplicate and related, but disconnected, data needing consolidation to address specific business requirements. The firm's goal was to generate consistent, absolute returns in all market conditions.

In addition, the firm was locked into one prime broker relationship. As the fund's strategy was increasingly spread across multiple asset classes, there was increasing concern about diversifying exposure and credit risk across multiple counterparties, protecting the trading intellectual property by diversifying across several prime brokers, and negotiating better terms (such as rates, stock availability for shorting, technology, etc).

Challenges
The fund faced the following challenges in advancing to a multi-prime broker environment:

- more points of contact and interfaces (multiple accounts) with the second and third prime broker;
- additional documents/counterparty monitoring;
- portfolio aggregation and reporting challenges;
- reconciliation with multiple primes putting pressure on systems and staff;
- trade booking and allocation becoming more complicated;
- increased error rate in the back office.

The client could also no longer rely on its single prime broker to satisfy their technology needs, and complementing their prime broker's service with a series of spreadsheets that tracked and managed operations and daily needs was no longer adequate.

At this point, what was necessary was a "leapfrog" of technology to match the growing demand.

Typically, a multi-prime broker hedge fund requires avenues to execute trades with the different brokers it deals with, along with an aggregated real-time P&L view of its portfolio. In addition, it needs a way to consolidate all trades into a centralised accounting system – and the ability to create daily performance and attribution reports. For this, spreadsheets simply do not work. Technology infrastructure is required to support its business needs.

Benefits of Implementing the System

Paladyne helped the firm in all aspects of its business. The firm used the PALA-DYNE suite of products in these areas:

- Paladyne Portfolio Master – The front office now has a way to capture trades from multiple trade execution systems and allocate them across its internal funds, in addition to having a real-time portfolio view it can slice and dice by various dimensions to show the P&L and aggregated positions.
- Paladyne Analytics Master – The middle office can now perform complex analytics on the portfolio and can generate various exposure reports to better assess its risks. Additionally, it can communicate trade files to counterparties as well as reconcile its daily books and records to each counterparty.
- Paladyne Security Master – The middle- and back-office now maintain their securities consistently in a global repository.
- Paladyne Price Master – In addition, the back office now prices its multi-strategy portfolio on a daily basis.
- Advent Geneva – The back office now maintains its aggregated books and records to shadow its fund administrator's work, while producing a daily NAV report.

The hedge fund manager accelerated their business performance in many ways:

- Improved performance through real-time awareness of key performance metrics.
- Increased investor satisfaction with timely comprehensive reports.
- Improved investor confidence with a robust infrastructure that addresses their front-, middle- and back-office needs.
- Streamlined and automated back-office processes to produce daily P&L and performance reports.
- Improved ability to view portfolio positions to initiate complex queries into portfolios – and across portfolios – by security, industry, customer, fund, strategy, trader or any other valid criterion.

Green IT

Introduction

CO_2 emissions, or rather the reduction of them, are getting higher on both the economic and political agendas of world leaders. According to experts, climate instability and global warming as well as CO_2 emissions are becoming the key expressions characterising what is considered to be the most significant threat to mankind and the environment.

Rising energy costs and increasing environmental damage are responsible for significant increases in the cost of living, and will continue to raise the costs of business. If prime brokers want to operate as green entities they should be prepared for the substantial and expensive changes that are involved.

According to industry sources, eminent scientists have shown clear evidence that there is an obvious relationship between the level of CO_2 in the atmosphere and planet surface temperature, i.e. the "greenhouse effect" that is characterised by more heat from the sun being trapped at higher CO_2 concentrations. Sir Nicholas Stern's report, the Stern Review,[63] showed that the level of greenhouse gases in the atmosphere before the industrial revolution was 280 parts per million (ppm) CO_2 equivalent (CO_2e), while the 2006 levels were around 430ppm CO_2e. It recommended that the level should be restricted to 450–550ppm CO_2e and that anything higher than this could heighten the risk of the impact of CO_2 emissions. The report also warned that the cost of stabilising CO_2 levels at 550ppm will be about £200bn or 1% of GDP per year and that this figure will rise as world GDP increases, and could be three to four times its size by 2050.

Other experts have also suggested that it may be impossible to reduce the growth in CO_2 emissions appreciably to avert an environmental disaster. The parties deemed responsible for the catastrophe will be expected to shoulder the responsibility with respect to cost as well as blame.

How does this relate to IT?

In recent times, the IT function in all business sectors has come under the spotlight as an area where significant energy savings can be made, with some experts convinced that IT may become a polluter on the scale of Sports Utility Vehicles (SUVs) and aircraft. IT in prime brokerage is no exception.

All aspects of IT nowadays have to factor power consumption into both operational and strategic decisions. It is only a matter of time before clients will start demanding to know the green credentials of the IT function.

Business Justification for a Green IT Strategy

The IT function in general is tasked with increasing business productivity and efficiency as well as reducing costs. As stated earlier, the prime brokerage business is becoming increasingly competitive and one way to remain competitive is to cut costs. Green computing offers an avenue to cut costs, especially if consumption of electricity is effectively reduced.

Adopting a power-based IT optimisation strategy is a medium for a prime broker to boost its green credentials in the face of the rising costs of energy and

---

63 This is a report that was compiled for the UK government by Sir Nicholas Stern, a British economist and academic.

infrastructure. This entails making power consumption an integral part of an IT policy that cuts across all of the processes that support a prime broker's workflow.

The approach taken to ensure that the IT function is more environmentally friendly will depend on the other internal policies of individual prime brokers. Nevertheless, there are basic practices that every prime broker should adopt as building blocks to the implementation of their green strategies. These include decisions centred on whether to implement a distributed or centralised architecture and decisions regarding the purchase of hardware. For example, they may opt for LCD as opposed to CRT monitors for energy efficiency and PCs and servers that run on the new generation of dual-core processors that come with less power consumption than conventional processors and offer better performance. Other practices will be enforcing the use of power-saving modes on unused IT hardware such as printers and PCs, and even the switching off of these pieces of equipment after working hours.

Server consolidation and virtualisation can also help in reducing costs, given that a large server is used to replace several smaller machines. Power requirements are also reduced as well as the overall heat that is produced.

Green Facts

- **Fact 1** – Switching a PC off overnight and at weekends can save up to £53 (in the UK for instance) in electricity costs.
- **Fact 2** – A single PC in office mode generates 1.094 tonnes of CO_2 per annum, equivalent to the CO_2 produced by a single passenger flying from London to Cairo.[64]
- **Fact 3** – During a PC's life from manufacture to disposal, approximately 2 tonnes of CO_2 are generated. Up to 1 tonne of this amount is generated through usage over three years when the PC is switched on for 24 hours a day, 220 days a year.
- **Fact 4** – An office with 50 desktop PCs may generate up to 10kW of heat.
- **Fact 5** – Data centres require 0.5 to one watt of cooling power for each watt of server power used and a typical x86 server consumes between 30% and 40% of its maximum power when idle.[65]
- **Fact 6** – The EU disposes of nine million tonnes of electrical and electronic waste each year, much into landfill.

Figure 10.4 would provide a basis for prime brokers to consider implementing IT projects that would not only save costs but also enhance their environmental friendliness.

In the next section, a project that will provide building blocks to a green IT strategy will be discussed.

---

64 Green IT – The Next Burning Issue for Business, IBM Global Technology Services, January 2007.

65 Ibid.

Figure 10.4 Typical power consumption and electricity costs at different levels of usage[66]

365 days a year, 24 hours a day (No switch off)

	Desktop kWh	Display kWh	Desktop £	Display £	Total kWh	Total £
PC + Display	569	175	52	16	745	68

220 days a year, 24 hours a day

	Desktop kWh	Display kWh	Desktop £	Display £	Total kWh	Total £
PC + Display	343	106	31	10	449	41

220 days a year, 8 hours a day

	Desktop kWh	Display kWh	Desktop £	Display £	Total kWh	Total £
PC + Display	114	35	11	4	150	15

Financial benefit, per PC + display, per year	£53
CO_2 emissions reduction, per PC + display, per year	374 kgs/CO_2

Source: Computacenter

Building Blocks to a Green IT Strategy

A number of green initiatives have led to the conclusion that a green IT strategy should be based on a thoughtful big-picture strategy built on incremental steps towards a cleaner, more energy efficient and environmentally friendly IT department.

Baselining Current Environmental Impact

For a prime broker that is seeking to create a green IT strategy, it is prudent to start the process by baselining the firm's impact on the environment from an IT standpoint. Obviously the main aim is to reduce energy consumption, therefore cataloguing improvements and planning future energy requirements is essential as is the grasp of the footprint of the IT environment.

Creation of a detailed baseline of the environmental impact of IT is invaluable to the execution of a green IT strategy as it allows decision makers to assess their existing capabilities. In addition, a detailed understanding of current procedures will provide a picture of the trade-offs and the likelihood that a green objective will take precedence over a cost or performance objective. Furthermore, the baseline will be instrumental in the estimation of the return on investment of any proposed green initiatives.

---

66 This is based on a desktop PC consuming 65 watts and an LCD display consuming 20 watts.

Phase 1 – Analysing energy consumption

The energy consumption baseline based on the current IT hardware of the prime brokerage function in an investment bank is a good starting point of the baselining process. There are essentially two methods for creating this energy consumption baseline.

1. Creating a mathematical estimate of energy consumption

This involves taking a current IT asset inventory and using this to calculate total energy consumption.

The following is an illustration using the prime brokerage arm of BizGroup, a fictitious American investment bank.

An audit of the prime brokerage arm's IT assets shows that it has 500 PCs, 80 laptops, 20 servers, 35 printers and 20 scanners.

The energy consumption for these IT assets can be estimated using a standard energy calculator. Figure 10.5 shows the total energy consumption of the IT assets for 1 year and a 4-year cumulative.

Figure 10.5 Total Energy Consumption

Hardware	Number of Units	National Energy Rate $USD / KWh	Energy Consumption (1 year)		Energy Consumption (4-year cumulative)	
			KWh	Cost (USD$)	KWh	Cost (USD$)
PCs	500	0.035	294,000	10,290	1,176,000	41,160
Laptops	80	0.030	47,040	1,411	188,160	5,645
Servers	20	2.000	11,760	23,520	47,040	94,080
Printers	35	0.010	20,580	206	82,320	823
Scanners	10	0.005	5,880	29	23,520	118
Total			379,260	35,456	1,517,040	141,826

Figure 10.5 does not include the energy consumption of air conditioners used to cool the servers.

2. Utilising software that manages the PC energy settings at network level

This involves using software that provides a more accurate picture of energy consumption in the prime brokerage arm based on actual user behaviour. This type of solution can be sourced from energy providers in the region that the prime brokerage arm operates in.

In order to obtain accurate results, it is advisable to factor in the heating, cooling and ventilation needs of the corporate network. This is particularly important in an age where most banks are moving away from distributed computing to the data centre. Experts have asserted that consolidation and centralisation have become the norm in recent times. In the IT industry, there is a general consensus that within a data centre/server environment, technological improvement is driving requirements for greater energy input to the building, for increased floor area and for increased cooling capacity.

According to IBM, this may be counter-intuitive, given the popularity of blade servers that are touted to allow the more efficient use of data-centre floor space, by packing more high-performance servers into a single rack.

It can be concluded that this will result in an increase in computing power and server numbers for a specified floor area, multiplying cooling problems, given that air is an inefficient media for cooling computers and empty space alone is insufficient to provide ample cooling. Air conditioning and other cooling techniques are required to keep temperatures in check. A typical 1980s server could be cooled quite easily. However, it is more difficult to cool a modern server as it requires more space around it, despite the fact that it takes up less floor space. While a modern server requires less power per unit of computing power, its general energy requirements will be significantly higher, and the need for improved cooling will further increase energy requirements – and naturally the environmental impact.

According to IDC, 48% of every dollar spent on a new server goes to power and cooling, while analysts at Gartner suggest that by the end of 2008, 50% of data centres will not have sufficient power to meet the power and cooling requirements of the new equipment used in high-density server environments.

Phase 2 – Cataloguing disposal practices

The current hardware disposal practices have to be catalogued in the next step in the creation of the footprint baseline. An item to be included in the catalogue is the option of using a certified IT hardware recycler that is responsible for ensuring that the toxic and hazardous materials inside the PC or monitor are disposed of in a environmentally friendly manner. This is particularly important in an age where the risk of misuse of sensitive data may result in contravention of regulations such as the Sarbanes-Oxley Act.

Using a certified IT hardware recycler is beneficial as these companies usually ship decommissioned hardware such as PCs to their facilities where they perform several subsequent disk wipes and test all components of the PCs. The catalogue may contain polices regarding useable PCs, such as how they may be made available for reuse by current employees, donated to charity, or refurbished and sold on the market. Unusable equipment can be taken apart for whatever useable parts can be sold, and the rest is recycled where possible so the materials can be used in other products.

The level of participation in the server manufacturer's disposal programme, where parts are returned to it for reuse whenever possible, should also be included in the catalogue as well as the resale or donation programmes to be put in place.

Phase 3 – Examining acquisition and hardware life cycle

This is the final step in creating the baseline and it involves cataloguing acquisition and PC life cycle practices. The prime brokerage arm needs to have a thorough understanding of the average lifespan of a PC in an organisation, which will help determine how to consider the environmental impact of manufacturing a PC. The average refresh cycle of the prime brokerage arm should be specified along with the current lifespan of the servers.

An advisable refresh cycle for desktop PCs is four years, based on the findings of recent studies on total cost of ownership (TCO). This means that hundreds of PCs have to be retired every month. Figures from the IDC show that in the USA, for instance, the installed base of PCs is expected to grow from 280 million in 2006 to 404 million in 2010, with 237.5 million PCs expected to be retired between 2005 and 2010. In 2006 alone, 30.7 million commercial PCs, or 70% of the total commercial installed base, were retired.[67]

It is worth noting, however, that an increasing number of retired PCs end up in landfills, creating higher toxic pollution. PCs and monitors, especially the old ones, contain a multitude of hazardous substances: lead, which can cause brain and kidney damage in children; mercury, which can cause nervous system and kidney damage; as well as cadmium, BFR (brominated flame retardants), and PVC (polyvinyl chloride), which are known to cause health problems such as cancer, respiratory illness, and reproductive damage and are able to accumulate in the human body and travel long distances through air and water when not disposed of properly.[68]

Also to be included in this phase are plans for any significant upgrades or replacements in the subsequent 12 to 24-month periods. The consideration the firm gives to green manufacturing practices during the purchasing process should be documented in this phase.

IT Practices that support a Green IT Strategy

After creating a baseline of the firm's current environmental impact from an IT perspective, the emphasis should be on identifying and focusing on some green IT objectives for the firm. For prime brokers, these objectives will be as a result of cost reduction and regulatory requirement as well as obligations towards social responsibility.

It should be noted that prime brokers that seek to operate as green entities should be aware of trade-offs along the way in the sense that the green approach may not be that green in the end. For example, if the main objective is to replace existing desktops with those that operate more energy efficiently to reduce environmental unfriendliness, the decision may actually be to keep current equipment and operate it more efficiently. According to a United Nations University 2004 study into the environmental impact of personal computers, around 1.8 tonnes of raw materials are required to manufacture the average desktop PC and monitor, and extending a machine's operational life through re-use holds a much greater potential for energy saving than recycling.

The study also showed that the manufacturing of one desktop computer

---

67 Erlanger, L., *Reap the Rewards of Hardware Recycling*, Infoworld, 12 July 2007.
68 Ibid.

and 17-inch cathode ray tube (CRT) monitor requires at least 240 kilograms of fossil fuels, 22 kilograms of chemicals and 1,500 kilograms of water. In terms of weight, the total amount of materials used is about equal to that of a mid-size car.[69] This means that the machine's lifespan is a significant factor in how green it is. The best way to minimise the impact on the environment from a personal computer therefore is to extend its useful life as much as possible. It is important that the prime broker understands the business driver behind an objective as this will help ensure that decisions made can meet objectives that are as green as possible.

PC power management

It would appear that the single greatest opportunity for reducing energy consumption for a prime broker is to implement a network-level PC power management solution.

Network-level PC power management

Networks pose special challenges for power management. Traditionally, most organisations have kept PCs on 24x7 and set operating system power management settings to monitor off or standby, – both of which consume almost as much power as a fully powered, idle machine. Historically, IT has had to grapple with an either–or decision with respect to PC power management. Desktop support analysts needed access to networked PCs for general maintenance and urgent security updates. Discrepancies between operating systems and software or network security issues made waking machines from a lower power setting, such as sleep or hibernate, inconsistent and unreliable. Network-level PC power management software solutions in conjunction with operating systems and software applications provide a solution to this problem.

Network-level PC power management solutions can allow prime brokers to implement policies that reflect user behaviour, accommodate IT maintenance needs and ensure a reduction in energy consumption for idle computers without impacting user productivity.

It is advisable to use a network-based solution to implement power-setting policies that reflect user behaviour and turn PCs to sleep or hibernate when not in use. An effective PC power management strategy can result in savings as high as US$60 per PC or even higher, depending on the regional charges for electricity. This saving translates into reducing carbon emissions by a considerable amount on an annual basis.

Extension of the useful life of IT hardware

If a prime broker chooses the option of extending the useful life of IT hardware, it might amount to a reduction in their environmental impact. Please note that the emphasis here is to extend the life of current hardware as opposed to replacing existing equipment with more energy-efficient products. A strategy that

69   William, M., *UN Study: Think upgrade before buying a new PC*, Infoworld, 7 March 2004.

focuses on replacement does not take into account the effect of manufacturing on the environment. According to industry experts, the amount of raw materials necessary to produce the average PC is equivalent to the amount of materials needed to build a mid-sized car.

Nevertheless, the following is a list of practices that help to extend the useful life of PCs and servers:

- Maintaining an optimum room temperature and humidity level in buildings where computers are used. For most PCs, room temperature should be between 15.5 and 29.5°C with a humidity level between 50 and 75% (to minimise any static build-up). For servers, ambient temperature should be around 20-21 °C.
- Ensuring that air quality is sufficient for circulation and prevention of overheating of the PCs.
- Electricity is a key factor in determining the longevity of PCs and servers. Putting policies in place to deal with electrical issues – such as brownouts, sags, outages, spikes and so on – is one of the ways to extend the useful life of IT hardware in general.
- Checking for updates for each application, such as Microsoft Office or Adobe Acrobat, using their in-built tools or via the support or download section of their websites.
- Cleaning temporary files, emptying the recycle bin and defragmenting PCs on a regular basis by using the utilities in the operating system.
- Requesting independent health checks on all systems and processes.

Implementing a green IT strategy is a challenging task for prime brokers, but not an impossible one. It can be realised through careful planning of future technology decisions and corporate initiatives that impact on the environment in the long term and ensure a company-wide change of mindset.

Commonly Used Terminology

This chapter contains a list of terminology commonly used in the prime brokerage industry.

Introduction

In an age when the prime brokerage business is becoming more lucrative for investment banks, it has become imperative for these firms to execute more IT projects to leverage technology as a source of competitive advantage.

To ensure success of these projects and the efficient use of IT as an enabler for the business, the functionality of the systems to be deployed has to accurately reflect the underlying business processes. Experts have continually asserted that there are no IT projects, just business projects and that the IT function brings technological advice to the table to help the business improve.

Nowadays, it is not uncommon to find that heads of IT in investment banks have a business background, that project teams are mixed – comprising business background and technical background people – and that IT leaders are being drafted into banks' elite decision-making circles.

Against this backdrop, IT professionals in prime brokerage need to be conversant with the terminology commonly used in the course of business activity in prime brokerage, from trading to securities lending and capital introduction.

Every industry has its own business terms. Prime brokerage is no exception. Below is a list of some of the terms used in the industry.

List of Terms

Accrued interest Coupon interest that is earned on a bond from the last coupon date to the present date.

Active premium The active premium is a measure of an investment's annualised return minus the appropriate benchmark's annualised return.

All-in dividend The sum of the manufactured dividend plus the fee to be paid by the borrower to the lender, expressed as a percentage of the dividend of the stock of the loan.

Alternative trading system (ATS) This is a trading venue where sellers and buyers of securities match their buy and sell order. It is termed as "alternative" because unlike an exchange, it is not regulated.

Arbitrage The process of buying and selling similar securities, commodities or currencies in order to profit from temporary price differentials between two markets.

Automated trading This is the type of trading whereby prices can be published and trades executed by IT systems.

Basis point One hundredth of a per cent or 0.01%.

Bearer securities Securities that are not registered.

Best execution This is the term used to describe the responsibility of brokers to provide the best price at order execution for their clients.

Beta A measure of a security's sensitivity to changes in the overall market.

Bilateral netting An agreement between two parties under which they exchange only the net difference between what each owes the other. The main aim is to reduce exposure to credit and settlement risk.

Black-box trading This terminology is used to describe the use of automated trading programs which seek to profit from market price swings, as well as arbitrage, between trading exchanges. Black-box trading systems, i.e. those running these types of program, are often used to determine optimal trading practices. These systems construct many different types of data, including buy and sell signals.

Blind broker A broker who acts as principal and does not give up names to either side of a brokered trade.

Bond Debt security that requires the issuer to pay the holder interest during the term of the bond, with some exceptions, and the principal at or before maturity.

Book-entry system[†] An accounting system that permits the electronic transfer of securities without the physical movement of certificates.

Book value Value computed from historical costs and expenses, using accounting rules rather than current market value.

Break a trade This is the practice whereby a long or short position in a security is unwound prematurely with respect to the intended trading strategy.

Buy-in A purchase of securities in the open market by a lender (or its agent) in order to replace loaned securities that a borrower has not been able to return.

Carry The interest cost of financing a securities inventory; may be either positive or negative.

Cash flow Net cash produced by an asset, as opposed to earnings calculated by accounting rules.

Cash trade A non-financing transition sale or purchase of securities.

Central securities depository (CSD) An institution for holding securities, which enables securities transactions to be processed by means of book entries. Physical securities may be immobilised by the depository or securities may be dematerialised (so that they exist only as electronic documents).

Cheapest to deliver The bond from among the deliverable bonds most likely to be selected for delivery into the futures contract.

Close-out (and) netting An arrangement to settle all existing obligations to and claims on a counterparty by one single net payment, immediately upon the occurrence of a defined event of default.

159

Closing (or back) leg[†] Second leg of a pair of transactions in the same securities, i.e. a securities lending transaction – one for a near value date, the other for a value date further into the future.

Cocktail swap A complex transaction based on several different types of swap and involving more than two counterparties.

Collateral pool A portfolio of securities, each with a specified yield (or yield formula) and expected term to maturity that is purchased by a lender with cash collateral received in connection with a securities loan.

Collateral yield The annual rate of return on a collateral portfolio, expressed as a percentage. Also referred to as reinvestment yield.

Composite A group of individual portfolios, retaining their original attributes, that are treated as a single portfolio for analysis.

Conduit borrower An intermediary in the securities lending chain, acting as principal, that borrows securities in order to lend them at a higher spread to another borrower whose credit may not be acceptable to the original lender or whose credit facility is filled with the original lender.

Corporate action This is a corporate event initiated by a company that brings about material changes which impact on its shareholders. In some cases, shareholders may or must respond to the corporate action or select from a list of possible actions. Typical events include spin-offs, mergers and stock splits.

Country code The code that identifies the country from which a security was issued.

Coupon The periodic interest payment on a security paid by the issuer to the holder, usually quoted as an annual percentage of the face amount.

Coupon frequency The number of interest payments made on an annual basis.

Cross border trading Trading that occurs between counterparties from different countries.

Cross hedge This is the practice of hedging a risk in a cash market security by buying or selling a futures contract for a similar, but not identical, instrument.

Custody risk This is the risk that occurs from the inability to hold secure custody of assets or the failure to obtain or release the correct secure custody when conducting purchase and sale transactions.

Dark liquidity pools These are private interbank or intrabank platforms used for trading in stock away from traditional exchanges.

Daycount method The method used to count the days in a month and the days in a year denoted as follows: (days in a month)/(days in a year).

Daylight exposure The risk that a market participant faces when related transactions are not settled simultaneously but at different times during the trading day, especially relevant when dealing in different time zones.

Decision price This is the price of a stock that informs the decision to buy or sell.

Dematerialisation[†] The elimination of physical certificates or documents of title which represent ownership of securities so that securities exist only as accounting records.

Depth of market This is the ability of the market to maintain relatively large market orders without affecting the price of the security.

Direct market access (DMA) This is a service offered by broker–dealers that enables clients to place buy and sell orders directly on electronic exchanges.

DK A questioned trade; a trade that is rejected because of some type of problem or operational error.

DV01 (Dollar value of .01) The approximate change in price (for $100 face value) for a one basis-point change in yield (0.01%).

Efficient portfolio A portfolio that provides the greatest expected return for a given level of risk.

Electronic communication network (ECN) An electronic system that is designed to remove the need for a third party in the execution of orders entered by an exchange market maker or an OTC market maker, and allows orders of this nature to be executed either wholly or partially.

Equity price risk The risk of loss incurred as a result of movements in equity prices.

Equity swap A swap transaction that involves an exchange of return on a recognised stock index or a specified basket of individual stocks for a fixed or floating rate of interest.

Escrow (securities lending) A service that involves collateral management services, including marking to market, repricing and delivery, by a third party.

Failed transaction A securities transaction that does not settle on the contractual settlement date.

Financial information exchange (FIX) protocol This is a series of messaging specifications for the electronic communication of trade-related messages developed for securities transactions and markets.

Free-of-payment delivery The practice in securities lending transactions whereby securities are delivered without corresponding payment of funds.

Funding rebate In securities lending transactions, this is the interest rate that a securities lender pays the borrower on cash collateral.

General collateral These are securities that are commonplace and used, in most cases, to collateralise cash borrowings.

Global custodian[†] A custodian that provides its customers with custody services in respect of securities traded and settled not only in the country in which the custodian is located, but also in numerous other countries throughout the world.

Global Master Securities Lending Agreement This is an agreement which is the market standard for securities lending of bonds and equities internationally.

Gross-paying securities[*] Securities on which interest or distributions are paid without any taxes being withheld.

Hedge The method for making offsetting commitments to reduce the impact of adverse movements in the price of a security.

High-touch trading This is a trading method whereby prices are quoted over the phone.

Implementation shortfall The difference between the decision price and the final execution price (including commissions, taxes, etc.) for a trade.

Income attribution This is the breakdown of total income by its sources.

Indemnification An agreement to compensate for damage or loss.

Index A statistical composite that measures changes in the economy or financial markets.

Indicative price (quote) Bid or offer price provided by way of information rather than as the level at which a trader is willing to trade. Indicative prices (quotes) enable a customer to plan a transaction but the transaction does not proceed until firm prices are provided.

Integrated portfolio A portfolio whereby funding and collateral portfolios are combined.

Interest rate risk This is the risk that the value of a security may be reduced as a result of change in interest rate levels.

Legal risk[†] The risk of loss because of the unexpected application of a law or regulation, or because a contract cannot be enforced.

Lendable assets An evaluation of the total market value of securities available for loan.

Liquidity The ease with which a security can be traded on the market.

Long position A situation where a security or contract is owned and the holder benefits from associated cash flows.

11. Commonly Used Terminology

Manufactured payments A payment received by the lender of securities in lieu of actual dividends or other income earned on the securities (net of any applicable taxes).

Margin call[*] A request by one party in a transaction for the initial margin to be reinstated or to restore the original cash/securities ratio to parity.

Market maker This is a firm that holds an inventory of a particular stock and is ready to trade this stock on a regular and continuous basis at a publicly quoted price. Each market maker vies for customer order flow by publishing buy and sell quotations for a guaranteed number of shares in their inventory. As soon as an order is received, the market maker immediately sells from this inventory or seeks an offsetting order.

Market price This is the last reported sale price of a security that is traded on an exchange or, if traded over the counter, its ask and bid prices in the open market.

Marking-to-market Revaluation of a security in a trade to current market values.

Matched book A portfolio of assets and portfolio of liabilities that have equal maturities.

Matching (or comparison)[†] The process for comparing the trade or settlement details provided by counterparties to ensure that they agree with respect to the terms of the transaction.

Migration risk This the risk that is associated with the possibility that a change in the credit quality of a security issuer will either increase or decrease the value of the security that it has issued.

Net paying securities[*] Securities on which interest or other distributions are paid net of withholding taxes.

New money The amount by which a replacement issue of securities exceeds the original issue (more money is raised for the borrower).

Onlend To borrow a security from one party and then lend the same security to another party.

Opening (or front) leg[†] First leg of a pair of transactions in the same securities, i.e. a securities lending transaction – one for a near value date, the other for a value date further into the future.

Open transactions Transactions that have no fixed maturity date and there is a chance that the transactions may be terminated or the rebate rate renegotiated on a daily basis.

Pair off[*] The netting of cash and securities in the settlement of two trades in the same security for the same value date. Pairing off allows for settlement of net differences.

Par Face value of a bond. Its value as it appears on the certificate or instrument.

Partialling* Market practice or specific agreement between counterparties that allows a part-delivery against an obligation to deliver securities.

Pay-for-hold* The practice of paying a fee to the lender to hold securities for a particular borrower until the borrower is able to take delivery.

Payup Cash required from the buyer to settle a trade. In a securities swap, payup is required when the securities bought are more expensive than the securities sold.

Policy effect The policy effect is the measure of the returns between a portfolio which sticks to a set guideline of investing vs one that takes a market neutral position.

Premium This is the fee charged by a lender on loans of securities against non-cash collateral.

Principal A party to a transaction that acts on its own behalf. In acting as a principal, a firm is buying/selling from its own account for position and risk, expecting to make a profit.

Proprietary trading* Trading activity conducted by an investment bank for its own account rather than that of its client when trading.

Real-time gross settlement (RTGS) The continuous (real-time) settlement of funds or securities transfers individually on an order-by-order basis (without netting).

Rebate rate The interest rate that a securities lender pays the borrower on cash collateral. This will normally be below the risk-free rate and will reflect the demand value of the securities. Also referred to as funding rebate.

Repricing The process of marking to market.

Risk adjusted return The return on a lender's lending activity based on the risks it took to generate the revenue.

Roll Renewal of a trade at its maturity.

Rolling settlement[†] A situation in which settlement of securities transactions takes place each day, the settlement of an individual transaction taking place a given number of days after the deal has been struck. This is in contrast to a situation in which settlement takes place only on certain days – for example, once a week or once a month – and the settlement of an individual transaction takes place on the next settlement day (or sometimes the next but one settlement day) following the day the deal is struck.

Screen-based trading Trading executed through a network of electronic terminals.

Securities settlement system (SSS) A system in which the settlement of securities takes place.

Settlement interval The amount of time that elapses between the trade date (T) and the settlement date typically measured relative to the trade date, e.g. if three days elapse, the settlement interval is T+3.

Shaping* A practice whereby delivery of a large amount of a security may be made in several smaller blocks so as to reduce the potential consequences of a fail.

Short sale (or short position)[†] A sale of securities which the seller does not own and thus must be covered by the time of delivery; a technique used (1) to take advantage of an anticipated decline in the price or (2) to protect a profit in a long position.

Solvency risk The risk of loss owing to the failure (bankruptcy) of an issuer of a financial asset or to the insolvency of the counterparty.

Special collateral Securities that are in high demand in the securities lending market for specific reasons.

Specials Specific issues borrowed to fulfil trading strategies. These trades generally are made up of "on-the-run" government issues and are more in demand by borrowers; therefore, they carry lower rebate rates.

Spread In securities lending, the difference between the rate of investment of cash collateral and the rebate rate of a loan; in investments, the difference between bid and asked price on a security or the difference between yields on or prices of two securities that have different characteristics or maturities.

Spread trade A structured transaction wherein a security(ies) is/are placed on loan, and simultaneously the cash received is invested in a short-term investment. Generally both sides, loan and investment, are entered into with the same party. The investment and loan transaction "mirror" each other in terms of reset, pay down and final maturity.

Straight-through processing The automated end-to-end processing of trades which entails the automated completion of trading life-cycle activities such as confirmation, generation, clearing and settlement of instructions.

Subcustodian A custodian bank that is responsible for safekeeping of securities within a single country and in only one currency. In contrast, a global custodian manages a network of subcustodians in order to perform custody operations for its clients worldwide.

Substitution* The practice in which a lender of general collateral recalls securities from a borrower and replaces them with other securities of the same value.

Takeout The cash balance on hand as of the final settlement date.

Term repo* A repurchase agreement that extends for a period of time longer than overnight; the repurchase agreement may, as an example, have a maturity of 7 days, 30 days, 2 months, etc.

Term transactions[†] Transactions with a fixed end or maturity date.

Thin market* A market in which trading volume and issue liquidity are low and in which bid and asked quote spreads are wide.

Third-party lending* A system whereby an institution lends directly to a borrower and retains decision-making power, while all administration (settlement, collateral, monitoring and so on) is handled by a third party, such as a global custodian.

Tick The standard minimum pricing unit in a particular market.

Time-weighted average price (TWAP) This is the average price of contracts or shares over a specified time. High-volume traders use TWAP to execute their orders over a specific time so they trade at a price that reflects the true market price. TWAP orders are a strategy of executing trades evenly over a specified time period.

Trade blotter A log of trades and the details of the trades made over a period of time (usually one trading day). The details of a trade will include such items as the trade date, price, order size and a specification of whether it was a buy or sell order. Trade blotters are used to carefully document the trades so that they can be reviewed and confirmed by the trader or the prime broker.

Trading desk A dedicated desk in an investment bank or brokerage firm where transactions for buying and selling securities occur.

Tranche A portion of a loan facility or share issue.

Tri-party repo[†] Repo in which bonds and cash are delivered by the trading counterparty to an independent custodian bank, clearing house or securities depository that is responsible for ensuring the maintenance of adequate collateral value during the life of the transaction.

Unmatched book (open book, short book)* When the average maturity of a bank's or a portfolio's assets exceeds the average maturity of its liabilities.

Volume weighted average price (VWAP) This is a trading benchmark that is often used in algorithmic trading. VWAP is calculated by summing up the dollars traded for every transaction (price multiplied by number of shares traded) and then dividing by the total shares traded for a particular day.

---

*   Source: "An Introduction to Securities Lending" ©Mark C. Faulkner.

†   Source: "Securities lending transactions: market development and implications"
    ©International Organisation of Securities Commissions and Bank for International
    Settlements. 1999 All rights reserved.

The Future

This chapter contains a discussion on the future of IT and business in the prime brokerage industry.

The Future: What does it hold for IT and Business in Prime Brokerage?

As seen from previous chapters, the business of prime brokerage is unique. Therefore, the future of the prime brokerage industry in business and IT is difficult to predict, given the overlap of the business activities of hedge funds and the investment banks that own most prime brokers, and their dependence on the fortunes of hedge funds.

However, what is certain is that competition in the industry will intensify in the years to come as banks will be vying for a slice of the market and the established players will be under pressure to differentiate their product offerings. In addition, there will be more pressure on the commissions that prime brokers charge and the spreads they enjoy on services such as margin lending and stock loans.

The meltdown of the Bear Stearns prime brokerage business (once ranked third among prime brokers globally) in 2008 resulted in many hedge fund clients hedging their bets by arranging relationships with other prime brokers and in some cases closing some of their funds. It remains to be seen how clients and other prime brokers react in the event of the collapse of another major player in the prime brokerage industry.

On the IT side, the prime brokerage industry will be looking to technology to help them "lock in" some of their clients. Most hedge funds do not have the budget to invest in technology that supports their complex strategies and have traditionally relied on prime brokers in this respect. The future revenue streams of prime brokers, as they seek to sustain relationships with their clients, could be dependent on how they utilise their existing technology or embrace forthcoming technological advancements.

That said, the following are factors that will shape the future of IT and business in the prime brokerage industry.

Globalisation of Hedge Funds

Hedge funds are usually perceived as the drivers of the improved liquidity in the global financial markets. Hedge funds are, in fact, a product of globalisation.[70] According to Sławiński (2006): *"This is because the global financial market with its diversity of liquid markets is a natural environment for hedge funds, enabling them to conclude reciprocal (arbitrage) transactions in many different markets. Only liquid markets provide possibilities for conducting short-term transactions without the risk of being trapped in a specific market."*

The statement above highlights the importance of globalisation in the hedge fund industry. But hedge funds, in the quest for globalisation, need to invest in markets that offer a combination of diversification benefits, large eco-

---

70 J. Loeys, L. Fransolet, "Have Hedge Funds Eroded Market Opportunities?" JPMorgan Chase, London 2004, p5.

nomic growth prospects and low interest rates. In our opinion, emerging markets fulfil these requirements, at least in the long term. Hedge funds focusing on emerging markets grew over tenfold from USD$2.6 billion to nearly USD$32 billion between October 1998 and November 2006.

Figure 12.1 Global GDP as % Year on Year

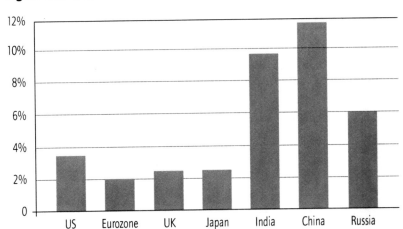

Source: Bloomberg

Industry reports show the sustainability of the long-term prospects of major emerging markets such Russia, China and India (See Figure 12.1).

Corporate profits have been exceeding expectation in recent times and the market fundamentals have been healthy. In addition, floating currencies, trade boom, paid-off currency debt, disciplined fiscal policies, and improved corporate governance and earnings are factors that contribute to the overall health. WTI Crude Oil prices rising from about $62 per barrel in July 2007 to around $120 barrel in June 2008 have been profitable for developing countries such as Russia, Mexico, Brazil and Venezuela.

In the quest for above-market returns, hedge funds are looking outside informationally efficient markets to seek arbitrage opportunities in the equity and bond markets of developing countries, i.e. the emerging markets. These markets offer spot price anomalies and also higher volatility and, as a result, hedge funds seek to exploit price trends.

The globalisation drive of hedge funds needs support from prime brokers that have a global reach; therefore prime brokers will need to assess their capabilities across the prime brokerage product range and in individual markets.

Increasing Client Demand

Increased competition amongst prime brokers and the thinning of margins have led to hedge fund clients increasingly demanding a lot more from their existing prime brokerage relationships, in the conventional areas as well as in the expanded, multi-prime services. Prime brokers, in response, have to make giant strides towards improving the quality of existing services in concert with expanding their range of offerings.

It can be argued that the trend toward the use of multiple prime brokers by hedge fund clients is largely due to the need for an expanded range of services. It is widely acknowledged in the industry that the demand for the following conventional services will increase in the future:

- **Securities lending** – As hedge fund managers become increasing dependent on their prime brokers for securities lending facilities, prime brokers will endeavour to include a wider range of securities in their inventories to lend to their hedge fund clients and earn more revenue from the premium charged.
- **Global coverage** – As stated earlier, there are investment opportunities for hedge funds in emerging markets and they are keen to exploit these opportunities. In their quest for global expansion, they will demand that their prime brokers have sufficient coverage of these markets in order to support their activities.
- **Access to increased returns** – Prime brokers will be pressurised by their hedge fund clients to provide new trading ideas, emanating from functions within their parent bank's research units or structured product groups. These trading ideas will enable hedge fund managers get the best out of their increasingly diverse and complex trading strategies.
- **Risk mitigation** – In the face of increased due diligence pressures, hedge fund managers have had to factor in counterparty risk, which in turn has led to the trend of utilising multiple prime brokers. In addition to the mitigation of counterparty risk, utilising multiple prime brokers can also aid in mitigating other risks such as liquidity, financing and operational risks.
- **Inclusion of OTC derivative products** – As the hedge fund industry has continued to expand and its strategies diversified to include derivatives, prime brokers have needed to add OTC products to their product scope to allow clients to continue to streamline their operations.

  Clients will derive benefits from the continued extension of OTC derivatives to the portfolio of products that prime brokers support, especially margin efficiency and operational reliability. Such benefits should give clients the confidence to diversify further into derivative products if they are appropriate for their trading strategies.
- **Infrastructure and technology** – Clients rely on prime brokers to offer them bundled front-to-back office technology and expect their prime brokers to not only invest currently in infrastructure and technology, but demonstrate the desire to continue to do so in the future.

Commoditisation of Prime Brokerage

It is safe to argue that commoditisation of prime brokerage has begun in earnest. Some industry watchers assert that with the myriad of prime brokerages, it can be tough to differentiate among the players, lending credence to this argument. Others believe that the recent trend among prime brokers of lowering their costs in order to attract new clients, and at the same time reducing complexity, will enhance the capabilities of their clients to switch, turning their service offerings into, essentially, a commodity. In addition, most investment banks already have the resources to enter the prime brokerage business; therefore, in terms of the range of services on offer, there will be very little to differentiate among them. Even if a prime broker introduced a new service, it would not be long before other prime brokers, at least the larger ones, followed suit because they would probably have the resources in place to provide the same service; therefore the differentiation element will not be sustainable.

Nevertheless, there are still ways in which commoditisation can be circumvented in the future and that is mainly through the quality of service and level of support provided to hedge fund clients. Prime brokers that give hedge funds the right kind of advice can make a difference between their success and failure, i.e. mitigating their business risk. According to industry sources, in recent times 50% of hedge fund failures are the result of not being able to run a business; i.e. weak infrastructure and poor operational management.

In conclusion, even if prime brokerage becomes an increasingly commoditised product, it is unlikely that its significance in generating revenue for investment banks will also become a commodity. Prime brokerage activities have been generating vast fortunes for investment banks in recent years and are expected to continue doing so in the foreseeable future.

Consolidation of the Hedge Fund Sector

By Ann C. Logue

Hedge funds benefit from scale; and the bigger, the better. There are approximately 9,500 hedge funds in the market, but most of the industry's assets are controlled by the 100 largest firms. Smaller funds seem to be more nimble when they trade and can look larger when necessary by using leverage, but they have an enormous disadvantage when it comes to maintaining a steady operating business. A small fund can be left without enough of a cushion to last a down year.

The standard compensation system is the so-called "2 and 20", in which the fund manager receives 2% of assets as a management fee, then takes 20% of the fund's profits each year. For a $100 million fund that returns 15%, the management fee would be $2 million and the performance bonus would be $3 million. That's not bad money, but office space, salaries and employee compensation can quickly eat into that. Even worse, if the fund doesn't make any money the next year, the fund manager receives just the 2% management fee, losing the revenues from the performance bonus. That might not be enough to keep the business in operation. Meanwhile, the fund with $1 billion in assets will earn a management fee of $20 million and a performance bonus of $30 million, and not all of its expenses will be 10 times higher than those of the fund that's a tenth the size.

The fluctuating revenue complicates employee compensation. A fund might not earn its performance bonus, but those staff members who did well with their slice of the money might resent not receiving bonuses for their contributions. A larger fund has a greater ability to attract and retain employees by offering less risk for those who perform.

Consolidation offers three advantages. First, it creates larger funds that receive a bigger stream of predictable revenue. Second, economies of scale can reduce the amount of expenses that the revenues need to cover, leading to better profits. Third, it makes the business more attractive to prospective employees, who see potential opportunities to manage their own slice of money and enjoy reliable pay for their performance at a larger firm.

Along with the operating efficiencies enjoyed by larger hedge funds, many hedge fund management firms have been going public. This not only allows them to get larger more quickly and diversify their market exposure, but it also makes them accountable to outside investors who want to see growth. A quick way to post increases in revenues and assets under management is to acquire hedge funds. Public stock makes fund acquisition easier, too, because the shares can be used as acquisition currency. And that public stock can be used to give employees ownership, stock options and other forms of compensation in addition to their fluctuating bonuses. Two of the public hedge fund companies that have been doing this successfully are Man Group and GLG. In addition, many large investment banks have been buying percentages of hedge funds; Alpha Magazine ranked JPMorgan Chase Asset Management as the largest hedge fund in both 2007 and 2008, in large part because of the partial stakes that the firm has in many successful funds.

To date, most of the acquisition activity has involved fund management companies buying funds. The next frontier will be roll-ups of hedge funds themselves, in which one fund will consolidate several smaller ones. It might be a little harder to get fund investors to agree, but it would help some small funds compete against their big brethren.

Evolution of Hedge Fund Business Model

One area that exemplifies the evolution of the hedge fund business model in recent times is the increase in activity of hedge funds in the secondary debt market. Industry reports estimate trading in loans by hedge funds in Europe has doubled in each of the years between 2004 and 2007. Hedge funds have traditionally bought distressed debt, but nowadays they have also started acquiring higher-quality corporate loans.

Investment banks are also willing participants in this trend. They sell loans to hedge funds in order to reduce their exposure and spread risk across the financial system. If this trend is sustained, banks will, in future, become more like middlemen in the lending market, arranging and packaging loans that they sell on to hedge funds.

Hedge funds are now competing with investment banks for financing traditional companies, transactions such as mergers and acquisitions, and leveraged buyouts by originating loans directly. A typical example is the financing of the purchase of Manchester United Football Club by Och-Ziff Capital Management Group, a hedge fund, in the form of payment-in-kind notes.[71]

This trend throws up issues in the relationship between prime brokers and hedge funds, given that on one hand prime brokers provide financing to hedge funds and on the other hand their parent investment banks will be selling loans to the same hedge funds. Furthermore, the smaller hedge funds might not have the resources to invest in technology to support their lending activities and might have to rely on prime brokers to provide the required technological platforms.

If the move of hedge funds to origination of loans becomes a fundamental change as opposed to a faddish development, then it remains to be seen how this will test the relationship between hedge funds and prime brokers in the future.

Increasing Use of Technology as a Differentiator

As prime brokers will be looking to differentiate their product offerings to their clients, technology could be the cornerstone of their differentiation strategies. Their hedge-fund clients continue to trade complex financial instruments and in doing so have propelled technology up their business agenda. Market developments have also meant that automation has become much more of a business process rather than a technology issue. Thus, they require automation within the back office that can now serve as a competitive advantage, demonstrating the dedication to efficiency and cost saving that their investors demand.

Since a number of hedge funds rely on their prime brokers for back-office processing, the efficiency and cost savings they offer clients could be a source of differentiation and competitive advantage. For example, a prime broker that can process a vanilla equity trade at $3 offers more cost saving to a client than a competitor that processes at $4 a trade. In addition, back-office processing efficiency is important to hedge funds as they are one of the biggest investors in exotic instruments. Investment in these instruments drives the creation of new strategies and increased complexity that require greater automation to support the continuing development of front-office activity.

71 Hilton, A. "Coming Soon: The Bank Loan you get from a Hedge Fund", *The Evening Standard*, 7 September 2006.

There are compelling reasons why automation, if used effectively, can be a source of differentiation for a prime broker. First of all, in the new paradigm of multiple prime broker relationships, the prime broker that can use automation to provide the most accurate audit trail to keep track of trade details for a hedge fund is most likely to win more business from hedge funds. Secondly, industry observers have stressed that automation has played a pivotal role in the recent trend of self-regulation advocated by regulators and governments for the hedge fund sector. Regulators in some jurisdictions around the world have chosen the option of best practice via the threat of regulation as opposed to a full-fledged mandate. For instance, in the USA the course of action as regards regulation was for the hedge fund sector to "self-regulate" through investors, which would entail both the hedge fund management company and investors adhering to a set of non-binding principles. Arguably, technology plays a key role as an enabler of this self-regulation, given that it can be used to reduce operational and systemic risk. In addition, technology and straight-through processing have assisted in the compliance with recommended best practices, such as transparency and audit trails, as well as the codes of conduct, thus preventing breaches of regulations.

The significant strides in middle- and back-office technology can be attributed to the advent of OTC derivatives and the hedge fund industry's insatiable appetite for exotic instruments. It would appear that the concept of siloed front and back office may become obsolete in the future. With innovation and the introduction of complex instruments, it is only a matter of time before the front, middle and back offices converge.

Furthermore, prime brokers looking to use technology as a differentiator could consider the following supplementary services to offer their clients in conjunction with conventional prime brokerage service offerings:

- **Open and independent technology architecture** – Hedge funds will require the requisite technology infrastructure to support their multiple relationships in the future and also a reporting functionality that is aggregated. In response, prime brokers must be adept at providing independent technology platforms that can integrate with the all of the prime broker's existing technology and also be open to the technology provided by any additional prime broker.
- **Independently hosted technology** – Prime brokers that get the delivery model of their independent technology offering right can use this as a differentiator. The delivery must be independent, third-party and offered as a full service Application Service Provider. The essence of the third-party delivery is to guarantee the privacy that hedge funds demand with respect to their trading strategies and positions. There are benefits in using a multi-prime technology delivered by an independent third party, given that it prevents the prime broker from having access to a fund's positions that it holds, and positions held by other prime brokers that the hedge fund manager has relationships with. Furthermore, there will be challenges in modifying and integrating a bank's internal system with other prime broker technology platforms.

Prime brokers that can take all the above points into account can leverage technology in the best possible way to achieve differentiation.

Conclusion

From our perspective, the future of the prime brokerage industry is bright and the revenue streams for the major players appear to be guaranteed for years to come. In spite of the difficulty of predicting the future of prime brokers, we believe that hedge funds and prime brokers will form a trusted partnership that will be based on a mutual desire to improve the levels and quality of service offerings. As hedge funds' requirements evolve, prime brokers will be able to integrate their respective technologies to meet these requirements and standard data communication protocols will help to increase service levels across the board.

In addition, if prime brokers are able to successfully service traditional asset managers, then prime brokerage could become one of the most profitable divisions of investment banks. This would present undoubted opportunities for IT professionals that are knowledgeable about the business activities in prime brokerage and how technology is used within the industry.

Appendix

List of Useful Websites

Bloomberg	www.bloomberg.com
Business Week	www.businessweek.com
Committee of European Securities Regulators	www.cesr-eu.org
Compliance Week	www.compliancenews.com
CNBC TV	www.cnbc.com
CNN	www.cnn.com
Dow Jones	www.dnb.com
European Central Bank	www.ecb.int
Financial Services Authority	www.fsa.gov.uk
Financial Times	www.ft.com
Fitch	www.fitchibca.com
Forbes	www.forbes.com
Fortune	www.fortune.com
Fund Action	www.fundaction.com
Greenwich Alternative Investments	www.greenwichai.com
Institutional Investor	www.institutionalinvestor.com
International Monetary Fund	www.isda.org
Ledbury Research	www.ledburyresearch.com
Luxury Institute	www.luxuryinstitute.com
London Stock Exchange	www.londonstockexchange.com
Moody's Investor Services	www.moodys.com
MorningStar	www.morningstar.co.uk
NASDAQ	www.nasdaq.com
New York Stock Exchange	www.nyse.com
Reuters	www.reuters.com
Scorpio Partnership	www.scorpiopartnership.com
Securitization News	www.securitizationnews.com
Security and Exchange Commission	www.sec.gov
Stonehage	www.stonehage.com
The New York Times	www.nytimes.com
The Depository Trust and Clearing Association	www.dtcc.com
The Economist	www.economist.com
Thomson	www.thomson.com
The WealthNet	www.thewealthnet.com
Wall Street Journal	www.wsj.com
Washington Post	www.washingtonpost.com
World Trade Organisation	www.wto.org

Prime Broker Directory

Alaris Trading Partners	www.alaristrading.com
Banc of America Securities	www.bofasecurities.com
Barclays Capital Prime Services	www.barclayscapital.com
BMO Capital Markets	www.bmocm.com
BNP Paribas	www.bnpparibas.com
BTIG	www.btig.com
Citi Prime Services	www.citigroup.com
Credit Suisse	www.credit-suisse.com
Cuttone&Co.	www.cuttone.com
Deutsche Bank	www.deutsche.com
Dresdner Kleinwort Prime Brokerage	www.drkw.com
Fidelity Prime Services	www.fidelityprime.com
FIMAT	www.fimat.com
Fortis Prime Fund Solution	www.merchantbanking.fortis.com
Gar Wood Securities	www.garwoodsecurities.com
Goldman Sachs	www.goldmansachs.com
Grace Financial Group	www.gracefg.com
Greenwich Prime	www.greenwichprime.com
Hedge Fund Capital Partners	www.hedgecap.com
Jefferies &Co.	www.jefferies.com
JPMorgan Chase	www.jpmorgan.com
Kas Bank	www.kasbank.com
Lehman Brothers	www.lehman.com
M.S. Howells & Co.	www.mshowells.com
MAN Financial	www.mfglobal.com
Merlin Securities	www.merlinsecurities.com
Merrill Lynch	www.gmi.ml.com
Morgan Stanley	www.morganstanley.com
Natexis Bleichroeder	www.natexisblr.us
NewEdge	www.newedge.com
North Point Trading Partners	www.nptradingpartners.com
Penson Worldwide	www.penson.com
Pershing Prime Services	www.pershingprimeservices.com
RBC Global Prime Services	www.rbcgps.com
RBS Greenwich	www.rbsgc.com
RCM Prime	www.rcmprime.com
Saratoga Prime	www.saratogaprime.com
Scotia Capital	www.scotiacapital.com
SEB	www.seb.se
Shoreline Trading Group	www.shorelinetrading.com
SIP Prime	www.sip-prime.com
TD Securities Prime Brokerage	www.tdsecurities.com

Terra Nova Financial	www.tnfg.com
Triad Securities	www.triadsecurities.com
UBS	www.ibb.ubs.com

Useful Job Boards

Banking Technology Jobs   www.bankingtechnologyjobs.com
Career Center   http://jobs.careerzone.banktechnews.com
Career Center   www.finextra.com/finjobLIST.asp
Computer Weekly   www.computerweekly.com/Jobs
Cv Library   www.cv-library.co.uk
efinancialcareers   www.efinancialcareers.com
IT Job Feed   www.ciquery.com
Job Databases   www.jobdatabases.co.uk
Job Crawler   www.jobcrawler.co.uk
Jobserve   www.jobserve.com
Jobsite   www.jobsite.co.uk
Monster   www.monster.co.uk
Online Job Match   www.onlinejobmatch.co.uk
Planet Recruit   www.planetrecruit.com
The IT Job Board   www.theitjobboard.co.uk
Total Jobs   www.totaljobs.com

Bibliography

Aite Group LLC and Vodia Group LCC, "Shaking Up Prime Brokerage: Unbundling Securities Lending, Financing, and Derivatives Transactions", Aite Group Report 200510171.

Ambrosio, J., "Green IT: Popularity due to Savings or Morals?", *Computerworld*, 13 September 2007.

Amos, G. and Nolan, D., (2001), *Mastering Treasury Office Operations*, Pearson Education Limited.

Avellanet, J., "Five Steps to Extend Your Computer's Life". Available from www.techsoup.org/Learningcenter/hardware/page6006.cfm.

Bank of England, (2001), "The Foreign Exchange and Over-The-Counter Derivatives Market in the United Kingdom", Quarterly Bulletin, Spring.

Barrett, R. and Ewan, J., (2006), "BBA Credit Derivatives". British Bankers' Association.

Baum, S., "Bear Stearns Taps Rivals for Hedge Fund Services", *Financial News*, 27 September 2007.

Bollen, B., "They Created the Game – So They Invent the Rules", FTFM Prime Brokerage, 5 March 2007.

Brennan, B., (2007), "Emergence of 130/30 Creates Perfect Storm", Finalternatives Prime Brokerage and Administration, July.

Brennan, M., (2007), *Hedge Funds and Prime Brokers*, Risk Books.

"Brokerage IT Spending Expects to Grow 1.3% through 2011", *Wall Street Technology*, 23 April 2008.

City A.M., "Contract for Difference: Cashing in Assets You'll Never Even Buy", 13 May 2008.

Computacenter, "Products and Services Green IT Advisory Service Briefing Paper". Available from www.computacenter.com.

Dedicoat, C., "Powering Down", CNBC European Business, April 2007.

DiStasi, M., (April 2004), "Prime Brokerage and STP: Bridging the Gap", *AIMA Journal*.

Dymet, J. et al., (2006), "Deutsche Bank Prime Brokerage: Alternative Investment Survey", *Hedge Fund Journal*, pp28.

Euromoney, (30 October 2006), "Prime Brokerage Debate: The Race to keep up with Clients". Available from www.euromoney.com.

Euromoney, "Wind in their Sales", Guide to Prime Brokerage, 2006.

Faulkner, M., (2004), "Introduction to Securities Lending", Spitalfield Advisors.

Federal Reserve Bank of New York, Guide to FR2004 Settlement Fails Data. Available from www.newyorkfed.org/markets/pridealers_failsprimer.html.

Ferry, J., (2006), "Prime Time", Risk, February.

Finalternatives, (2008), "Prime Brokerage", June.

Finalternatives, "Institutions Show Appetite for Emerging Hedge Funds". Available on www.finalternatives.com.

Finalternatives, "Two Wall Street Giants Gain Ground in Prime Brokerage Space". Available on www.finalternatives.com.

Financial Times, "No Chance of Exclusive Relationship", FTFM Prime Brokerage, 5 March 2007.

Financial Times, "Pretenders to the Crown Set Out Their Stall", FTFM Prime Brokerage, 5 March 2007.

Foreign Exchange Committee, Foreign Exchange Prime Brokerage: Product Overview and Best Practice Recommendations.

Foreign Exchange Committee, Foreign Exchange Transaction Processing: Execution-to-Settlement Recommendations for Non-dealer Participants.

Francis, F., "The Role of the Prime Broker", Canadian Investment Review, Spring 2002, p39.

FT Mandate, "From the Back Office to the Trading Floor", 2006, September.

FT Mandate, "Set The Record Straight", 2006, September.

FT Mandate, "The Magic Hand of Triparty Repo", 2006, September.

Foreign Exchange Committee, Guidelines for Foreign Exchange Trading Activities, the Management of Operational Risk in Foreign Exchange.

Hughes, C., "Committed Entrants Can Break into Market", FTFM Prime Brokerage.

IBM Global Technology Services, (2007), "Green IT – The Next Burning Issue", January.

The Independent, "You Know the Finance Bomb is Ticking But How Big Will the Explosion Be?", 23 March 2008. Available from www.independent.co.uk/news /business/analysis-and-features.

Ivy Schmerken, "FX Prime Brokers Rally around Give-Up Trades", Wall Street Technology, 10 April 2003.

Kalwat, J., (June 2007), "Investing in 130/30 Strategies", Evaluation Associates.

Kim, K., (2007), Electronic and Algorithmic Trading, Elsevier Inc.

King, R., "Averting the IT Energy Crunch", *BusinessWeek*, 14 May 2007.

Loeys, J. and Fransolet, L., (2004), Have Hedge Funds Eroded Market Opportunities?, JPMorgan Chase, London. p5.

Mackintosh, J., "How a Fledgling has Spread its Wings", FTFM Prime Brokerage, 5 March 2007.

Mackintosh, J., "We Need to be Defensive as Offensive, Says the Man with a Bullseye on his Back", FTFM Prime Brokerage, 5 March 2007.

Madhavan, A., (2002), "Implementation of Hedge Fund Strategies", Hedge Fund Strategies, Autumn.

Maleshefski, T., "5 steps to green IT", eWeek.com, 12 October 2007.

MARHedge, (2005), "Cutthroat Competition: New Entrants Mean More Challenges for Prime Brokers, More Cost-Saving Options for Funds", Prime Brokerage Special Report, December.

Natajaran, N., "Prime Brokerage", Financial News.

O'Kane, G., (2006), "Prime Brokers Move to Exploit Demand", FT Mandate, December.

Robertson, M., (December 2006), "Prime Brokers Move to Exploit Demand", Financial Times Mandate.

Rush, D., "Echoes of the Past: LTCM Meriwether in Trouble Again", The Sunday Times Special Report, 25 May 2008.

Schultes, R., "Crisis Changes the Rules of the Game for Prime Brokers", Financial News, 9 April 2008.

Simotas, P., (2006), "Bringing FX Prime Brokerage to Currency Overlay", FX Concepts.

Sławiński A., "The Role of Institutional, Investors, Banks and Hedge Funds in the Development of the Global Financial Market", Paper for the conference, Contemporary Problem of International Finance, 2006.

Sturgeon, W., "Green IT: Do it for the money, if nothing else", CNET News.com, 27 November 2006.

Thind, S., "Prime Brokers see chance to encroach on custodial relationship", Financial News, 10 April 2008.

Underwood, S., "Dynamic IT Systems Can Give Prime Brokerage An Edge", FTFM Prime Brokerage, 5 March 2007.

Williams, M., "UN Study: Think upgrade before buying a new PC", IDG Newservice, InfoWorld, 7 March 2004.

Index

130/30 strategies 82–4
2 and 20 system 171–2

A

account reconciliation (FX) 97–8
accrued interest 123, 158
acquisition currency 172
acquisitions 17, 56
active premiums 158
agent prime brokerage 29
AIM 62
algorithmic trading tools 133
all-in dividends 158
allied industries 59–66
alternative investments 13
alternative trading system (ATS) 158
American Bankers' Association 67
application programming interface (API) 99–100
Application Service Providers 174
arbitrage trading 112, 158, 169
Asian markets 88–9
asset classes 78, 94
asset prices 110
assets
    hedge fund 12, 13, 15, 21–2, 23
    prime brokerage 5–6
assets under management (AUM) 21, 41, 48, 70, 172
audit trails 174
auto-borrow 43
automated trading 45, 99, 158, 159
autonomy from the trading division 34

B

back-office functions 27, 35, 36, 104, 173, 174
back-office technology 36, 45, 133, 134, 135, 170, 173, 174
Banco Espirito Santo 9
bank-issued letters of credit 118
Bank of America 9, 58
Bank of England 59–60
banking business lines 70–3
Barclays Capital 3, 9, 58, 59
Basel Committee on Banking Supervision 55
Basel II Accord 54, 55–6

basis points 5, 7, 119, 121, 126, 158, 161
Bear Stearns 5, 9, 58, 59, 71, 73, 168
bearer securities 158
best execution 55, 132, 133, 158
beta 45, 83, 159
bilateral netting 97, 115, 159
black-box trading 159
blind brokers 159
block trade execution 105
Bloomberg 63, 64
BNP Paribas 9, 58
BNY Mellon 58
bond-washing 111
bonds 4, 13, 14, 73, 103–4
book-entry systems 159
book value 159
borrower defaults 110
Borsa Italiana 62
break a trade 159
Breman, B. 39
Bretton Woods system 78
British Bankers' Association 74
business environments 54–68
buy-ins 35, 89, 125, 159
buy/sell backs 123, 126–7

C

Calyon Financial 9, 59
capital adequacy 55
capital introduction 31, 72
carry 159
cash as collateral 117, 118, 120–2
cash collateral reinvestment risk 130
cash equities 44
cash excesses 39
cash flow 29, 97, 98, 159, 162
cash management capabilities 35, 44
cash trades 159
CDS 49, 50, 77
Central Facility for Funds 65
central securities depositories (CSDs) 65–6, 115, 116, 120, 159
centralised securities clearing facility 2
certificates of deposits 118

185

CESR 60–1
CFD 13, 26, 44–5, 89–92, 112
charitable organisations 22
cheapest to deliver 159
Chinese Wall 104
CIBC World Markets 9
Citi Prime Services 10, 58, 59
clearance and settlement 28–9
clearing account with credit enhancement 2
clearing of securities loans 115
Clearstream International SA 65
client demand 170
client relationships
    with executing dealer 105
    with hedge fund manager 14
    with prime broker 105–6
close-outs 98, 159
cocktail swaps 160
codes of conduct 174
collateral 30, 48, 100, 111
collateral adjustments 115
collateral pool 160
collateral substitution 115
collateral yield 160
collateralisation 49, 50, 79
    foreign exchange 79
    multiple counterparties 49, 50
    over-collateralisation 51, 127
    pre-collateralisation 116
    securities lending 113, 117, 119–22, 125
    uncollateralisation 125
collateralised lenders 4, 32
Committee for European Securities Regulators see
    CESR
Committee on Uniform Securities Identification
    Procedures see CUSIP
commoditisation of prime brokerage 171
commodity funds 43
commodity pool 14
Commodity Trading Advisors (CTA) 18, 58, 95
Compensation Agreements 102
composites 160, 162
conduit borrowers 160
Confidentiality Agreement 37, 38–9
confirmation of FX transactions 96–7
confirmation of securities loans 114–15
connectivity 36
consolidation of the hedge fund sector 171–2
consulting services 31
consumer protection 55

contracts for difference see CFD
conversion privileges 117
convertible arbitrage 16, 110
convertible bonds 16, 118
corporate actions 31, 86, 135, 160
corporate bonds 112, 118
corporate loans 172
costs
    energy 149–50
    prime brokerage 47–8
counterparties 96, 100, 113, 125
counterparty risk 130, 170
country codes 67, 160
coupons 16, 74, 104, 122, 123, 158, 160
credit assets 73
credit crunch 57
credit default swaps 74, 77
credit derivatives market 44, 73–7
credit-limit monitoring 103
credit lines 31, 103
credit-linked notes 74
credit-related hedge funds 43
credit relationships 100
credit risk 50, 74, 125–8
credit risk mitigation 103
credit standing 113–14
Credit Suisse 5, 9, 58, 59, 135
cross-asset prime brokerage 94–107
cross border trading 56, 104, 160
cross-default clauses 50
cross hedge 160
currency 78
currency overlay 79–81
CUSIP 67, 68
custodian banks 88, 118
custody of assets 29
custody risk 160

D
Daiwa 3
dark liquidity pools 160
data aggregation 143–4, 145
data providers 63–5
daycount method 160
daylight exposure 116, 161
debentures 103
debt instruments 103
decision prices 161, 162
delivery by value (DBV) 118
delivery versus delivery (DVD) 115, 125

delivery versus payment (DVP) 115, 116, 125
dematerialisation 161
Dentskevich, Paul 41
Depository Trust and Clearing Corporation (DTCC) 77
depth of market 161
deregulations 111
derivatives
  to avoid disclosure 46
  for leverage 29–30
  positions 13
  support 31
Deutsche Bank 3, 9, 58, 59
direct market access (DMA) 86, 132, 161
dirty prices 122
disclosure obligations 46
disclosure requirements 14
distressed securities 17
diversification 15
dividend enhancements 47, 86
dividends, cash and stock 117
DK trades 43, 46, 51, 161
dot.com crash 90
Dow Jones Newswires 64
Dresdner Kleinwort 9
due diligence 45, 89, 170
DV01 45, 161

E

ECB 60
economic factors 41–51, 56
efficient portfolios 161
electronic communication networks (ECN) 99, 161
electronic foreign-exchange platforms 101
electronic prime-broker model 100
electronic trading platforms 45–6, 99
embedded credit derivatives 74
emerging markets 169, 170
employee compensation 172
endowments 14, 22
energy
  consumption baseline 152–3
  consumption by IT 150–1, 152–3
  costs 149–51
enhanced leverage 31
environmental factors affecting prime brokers 54–7
environmental impact of IT 151–4
equities 3, 44–5, 103, 118
Equity CFDs 91–2
equity-linked products 74
equity long/short 16, 17, 49, 110

equity price risk 161
equity-related hedge funds 43
equity repo 112
equity swaps 139, 161
Erlanger, L. 154
Escrow (securities lending) 161
eSecLending 7
EU Commission 60
EU framework directives 60
euro 60
Euroclear Bank SA 65–6
Euronext 62
Euronext.liffe 62
event-driven strategy 17
exchange rates 56
exchange traded contracts 26
exchange traded derivative instruments 26
exchanges 61–3
Executing Broker Agreements 37, 40
executing brokers/dealers
  client relationships 105
  credit risk mitigation 103
  and foreign exchange 94–5, 98–9, 100, 101
  give-up agreements 101–2
  and hedge funds 28–9, 40, 44
  relationship with prime brokers 26, 57, 84, 102, 104, 106–7
  and sub-accounts 106
execution management systems (EMS) 132
extended repo facility 46

F

failed transactions 128, 161
Faulkner, Mark C. 116, 120, 121, 123, 126–7, 166, 182
fees
hedge funds 18–19
prime brokerage 4–5
for stock loans 4
Fidelity Investments 9, 58
Fimat 59
financial crime 59
financial information exchange *see* FIX
Financial Services Authority *see* FSA
Financial Times (FT) 64–5
financing and margining 29
financing risks 170
FIX 36, 57, 161
fixed income 103–7
fixed income and derivative products 3
fixed income arbitrage 16

187

fixed income hedge funds 43, 49
fixed income prime brokerage 44, 104
fixed income securities 56, 103
Fleming, Michael J. 129
Foreign Exchange Committee (FXC) 102
foreign exchange prime brokerage *see* FX prime
    brokerage
foreign exchange trading 77
Fortis 10
forward FX 96
Four Ps 32–4
Fransolet, L. 168, 183
fraud 71
free-of-payment (FOP) 115–16, 161
front-office systems 36, 134, 135, 136, 174
front-to-back office technology 170, 174
FSA 40, 45
fund administrators 9, 27, 31, 81, 143–4, 145
funding rebates 161, 164
FundSettle 66
future for IT and business 168–75
futures 18, 43, 94, 104
FX prime brokerage 77–81, 94–5, 98–9
FX services (foreign exchange) 43, 44
FX swaps 79
FX trade process flow 95–8

G

gamma element 16
Garbade, Kenneth D. 129
general collateral 126, 162, 165
general collateral repo rate 129
give-up agreements 50, 95, 98, 101–2
give-ups 28, 40, 48, 51, 103
GLG 172
Global Custodian Prime Brokerage Survey 58–9
global custodians 58, 162, 165, 166
global financial markets 168
global hedge fund assets 5, 6
global hedge fund industry 21–2
global hedge funds 48
Global Master Repurchase Agreement *see* GMRA
Global Master Securities Lending Agreement 162
global prime brokerage
    brokers 59
    market 3, 5–9, 111
    market share 5, 6
    revenues 5–7, 8
global securities presence 35
globalisation of hedge funds 168–9

GMRA 49, 122
Goldman Sachs 3, 5, 10, 58, 59
government bonds 114, 118
Green IT 148–56
green mail transactions 17
gross-paying securities 162
gross pricing 43
growth/value/industry/geographical/
    capitalisation 17

H

haircuts 46, 114, 122
Hang Seng Index 88
hard-to-borrow securities 86
hardware
    acquisition 153–4
    disposal and recycling 153, 154
    life cycle 153–4, 155–6
hearsay reporting capabilities 143, 145
hedge 162
hedge fund managers 14, 21–2, 34, 172
hedge funds 2, 3, 9
    characteristics 14
    collateral requirements 2
    definition 12–14
    failure 171
    life cycle 5
    performance 15
    reasons for investing 15
    regulations for 13, 21
    relationship with prime brokerage 12, 26–40,
        41–51, 85–7, 173
    risk management 4
    risk reduction 15
    sources of investments 22–3
    strategies 5, 14, 15–18
    style allocation 15–16
    world's 10 best 19
high net worth individuals 14, 22, 23
high-touch trading 162
high-water mark 20
HMR&C 44, 45
hurdle fees 18–19
hypothecation 39, 47

I

implementation shortfalls 162
in-house IT systems 45, 144, 145
income attribution 162
indemnification 162

independently hosted technology 174–5
index 90, 91, 161, 162
index trades 74
indicative prices 162
initial margin, securities 114
initial public offerings (IPOs) 31, 56, 63, 112
institutional investors 21, 22–3, 32, 70
insurance companies 14
integrated portfolios 162
inter-settlement events (securities) 117
Interactive Brokers 10
interest payments 117
interest rate risk 16, 162
interest rate spreads on loans 4
interest rate swaps 104
interest rates 56, 60
intermediation 49–50, 77
internal financial auditing controls 55
international prime brokerage platforms 3
international securities 104
International Securities Number *see* ISIN
International Swap and Derivatives Association *see*
    ISDA
investment banks
    business environment 54
    and CFDs 92
    and foreign exchange 77, 78
    and hedge funds 72, 73, 172, 173
    and IT projects 142
    and prime brokerage 3, 4, 5, 9–10, 34, 37, 71,
        111, 171
    and securities lending 89
investment managers 88
investment professionals 14
investment protection 14
investment sources 22–3
investor protection standards 55
investors 55
ISDA counterparties 49
ISDA Master Agreements 37, 40, 49, 50
ISDA novation protocol 77
ISIN 67
ISO 6166 67
issuance access 31
IT asset inventory 152
IT projects 142–56

J
Jefferies & Company 10, 58
job boards 181

JPMorgan Chase 5, 10, 58, 59, 71, 73, 172
JWM Partners 57

K
Keelan, Brian 89

L
legal
    factors 57
    frameworks 101
    relationships 37–40
    risk 130, 162
    title 118–19
legs of transactions 117, 122, 125, 128, 160, 163
Lehman Brothers 10, 59
lendable assets 88, 162
lending agents 88
letters of credit 113, 118
leverage
    and 130/30 strategies 82
    and hedge funds 29, 30, 31, 35, 48–9, 90
    policy 4, 32, 34
LIBOR-based cash flows 74
limited partnerships 12, 13, 14
lines of credit 31, 103
liquidity 162
    and foreign exchange 79, 94, 100
    and risk controls 129–30
    and securities lending 87, 88, 110, 114, 116
liquidity risk 128, 170
loans 73, 74
Loeys, J. 168, 183
Logue, Ann C. 70, 171
London Stock Exchange (LSE) 61–2, 89, 90
long-only strategies 82
long position 27, 30, 82, 83, 89, 112, 162, 165
long/short equity 16, 17, 49, 110
Long-Term Capital Management 57, 111
lookback fee 20

M
Mackintosh, J. 4, 183
macro strategy 18
Main Market 61
Man Group 172
managed account swap 30
managed funds 18
management changes 17
management fees 18
manufactured payments 117, 163

margin 39
margin, securities 114
margin calls 38, 114, 163
margin financing, for leverage 29–30
margin relationships 50, 100
margins, prime brokerage 71–2, 81
market makers 111, 114, 161, 163
market neutral 17
Market Participants Consultative Panel 60–1
market prices 117, 122, 159, 163, 166
market repo rate 123
market risk 128
Markets in Financial Instruments Directive *see* MiFID
marking-to-market 130, 137, 163
master accounts 27
Master FX Give-Up Agreement 102
matched books 163
matching 95, 99, 106, 115, 163
material changes (securities) 115
material terms 98
maturity (securities) 113
merger arbitrage *see* risk arbitrage
mergers 17, 56
Mergers and Acquisitions (M&A) 112
Merrill Lynch 10, 58, 59, 71
middle-office systems 133, 134, 135, 136, 174
MiFID 54, 55
migration risk 163
miscellaneous fee 20–1
Monetary Policy Committee 59–60
money market instruments 118, 121
Morgan Stanley 3, 5, 10, 58, 59, 71
mortgage-backed securities 104
multi-asset trading 94
multi-prime brokerage systems 142, 143, 174
    case study 145–8
multi-strategy funds 15
multilateral netting 115
multiple counterparties 49, 76
multiple prime brokers 48, 73, 84–7, 133, 170

N

naked shorting 112
NASDAQ 63
National Association of Securities Dealers Automated
    Quotient *see* NASDAQ
National Numbering Agency *see* NNA
National Securities Identification Number 67
National Securities Identifying Number (NSIN) 67
NAV decline triggers 49, 50

net asset value (NAV) 18, 20
net paying securities 163
net pricing 43
netting 97
netting arrangements 115
network-level PC power management solutions 155
new money 21, 163
New York Stock Exchange 62
Newedge Group 10, 57
NNA 66, 67
non-equity securities 86
Nostro banks 97
novation 97
NYSE Arca 62
NYSE Euronext 62

O

offering materials 40, 47
Office of Revenue Commissioners 45
office space 31, 72
Official List 59
offshore funds 14, 21
OMX 63
onlends 163
onshore funds 21
open and independent technology architecture 174
open-ended funds investment 56
open transactions 163
operational efficiency 142–5, 172
operational risk 130, 170, 174
opportunistic strategy 18
order management systems (OMS) 106, 132
OTC derivatives 58, 170, 174
over-collateralisation 51, 127

P

pair offs 163
pairs trading 90
Paladyne Systems 134–5
    case study 145–8
par 164
partialling 164
pay-for-hold 164
payment-in-kind notes 173
payups 164
PBA
    benefits of 40, 50, 100
    description 39, 102
    legal requirements 37, 47
PC power management solutions 155

pension funds 14, 22, 23, 70, 95
performance bonuses 172
performance fees 18
Pershing 58
plain vanilla debt securities 104
planned trading strategies 88
policy effect 164
political environmental factors 54–5
portfolio financing firms 7–8
portfolio management 3
Powernext 62
pre-collateralisation 116
pre-trade preparation (FX) 96
premiums 73, 74, 98, 164, 170
pricing, securities 113
pricing analytics 133
pricing inefficiencies 16–17
pricing structures 81–2
prime brokerage
    as banking business line 70–3
    costs 47–8
    definition 2–3
    fee structure 4–5
    fees 71
    future 168–75
    global market 5–9
    history 3–4
    IT projects 142–56
    leaders 5, 6
    margins 71–2, 81
    relationship with executing brokers 106–7
    relationship with hedge funds 12, 26–40, 41–51, 85–7, 173
    revenues 71
    service providers 9–10
    systems used 132–9
    technology 133, 173–5
    trends 70–92
prime brokerage agreements *see* PBA
prime-brokered trade execution model 99–100
prime brokers 179–80
    products and services 26–32, 36, 43–4
    qualities 34–7
    role 26, 27
    single vs multiple 48
principal prime brokerage 29
principal risk (credit) 125
principals 7, 29, 33, 159, 160, 164
private banks 14
private pooled investment limited partnerships 13

product capability 36
Professional Securities Market 62
proprietary trading 36, 86, 96, 164
public stock 172

R
Rabobank 10
RBC Capital Markets 10, 58
RBS 10
real-time gross settlement (RTGS) 164
rebate rates 121, 163, 164, 165
record keeping 30–1
regulations
    hedge funds 13, 21, 54–5, 142, 174
    prime brokers 54–5, 59
    securities 113
regulators 59–61, 174
rehypothecation 47
relative value strategy 16
reorganisations 17
replacement cost risk (credit) 125, 128
reporting and statements 31, 36
repos 122–3, 126–7
    equity repos 112
    extended repo facility 46
    and fixed income 104
    repo market 44, 49, 116
    repo rates 113, 122, 123, 129
    reverse repos 123
    term repos 166
    tri-party repos 166
repricing 164
repurchase agreement *see* repos
Request for Proposal (RFP) 37, 38, 39, 42
Reuters Instrument Code *see* RIC
reverse repos 123
RIC 68
right to foreclose 119
rights issues 56
rights of distributions 117
risk adjusted return 164
risk analytics 32, 133
risk arbitrage 17
risk assessment matrix 32
risk controls 129–30
risk information flow 4, 32
risk management
    currency 79–80
    hedge funds 4, 32–4, 86
risk mitigation 103, 170

Business Knowledge for IT in Prime Brokerage

rolling settlements 164
rolls 164
Rush, D. 57, 183

S

Sarbanes-Oxley Act of 2002 *see* SOX
screen-based trading 164
SEC 40, 55, 61
secondary debt market 172-3
secrecy of industry 5, 13
Securities and Exchange Commission *see* SEC
securities lending 110-30
    collateralisation 113, 117, 119-22, 125
    comparison with repo and buy/sell back 126-7
    definition 30, 110
    fees 118 and more
    future demand 170
    and hedge funds 86
    history 110-12
    and interest rates 56
    market, evolution of 87-9
    revenue generation 7-8, 124
    risks 125-8, 129
    securities loan transactions 118-19
    settlement fails 129
    transaction life cycle 113-17
    types of transactions 117-24
securities regulators 60, 61
securities settlement system (SSS) 165
security identifier types 66-8
security interest 39
SEDOL 67-8
self-regulation 174
sell/buy backs 123-4
Selz, Furman 3
Service Level Agreement (SLA) 37, 40
settlement coverage 112-13
settlement fails, securities lending 129
settlement (FX) 97
settlement intervals 116, 165
settlement of securities loans 115-16, 117, 125
settlement period of securities loans 116-17
settlement risk 128
shadow reporting 36
shaping 165
shares 12-13, 59, 63, 67, 82, 90-1, 112
short sales 16, 17, 26, 27, 30, 110, 165
short selling 14, 17, 82, 83, 110, 111, 116, 129
shorting securities 110
Side Letters 37, 40

single counterparty 49
Single Market 60, 61
single vs multiple prime brokers 48
Sławiński, A 168, 184
social environmental factors 57
software vendors 134-9
solvency risk 165
source of Investments 22-3
SOX 54, 55, 153
special collateral 165
special collateral repo rates 129
special situations 17
specialised brokerage services 2
Specialist Fund Market 62
specialist regional players 111
specials 165
spin-offs 17
spread 4, 88, 114, 121, 160, 165
spread trades 165
stamp duty 44, 89, 90
Standard & Poor's 67
standard settlement instructions (SSIs) 97
standby letters of credit 113
start-up services 31, 142
statistical arbitrage 16, 111
Stern Review 149
Stock Exchange Daily Official List *see* SEDOL
stock markets 56
stock splits 117
stocks 15, 17, 35, 43, 46, 82
straight-through processing 45, 103, 105, 113, 165, 174
structured products 46
structures (hedge fund) 14
sub-accounts 105, 106
subcustodians 165
substitution 165
SunGard 135-7
surrender fees 18
swap trading 86
SWIFT 97, 114
synthetic prime brokerage 58, 86
systemic risk 174
systems used in prime brokerage 132-9

T

takeout 165
Takeover Code 46
tax arbitrage 111, 112
tax-efficient structures 46

tax harmonisation 112
TBMA/ISMA Global Master Repurchase Agreement
    see GMRA
technology
    capabilities of prime broker 36, 142, 144, 145
    independently hosted 174-5
    infrastructure 170, 174
    open and independent architecture 174
    prime brokerage market 133, 173-5
    technological advances 57
term transactions 166
terminations
    prime brokerage accounts 39
    securities loan 117, 122
The European Central Bank see ECB
thin markets 166
third-party securities lending agents 111, 166
third-party technology providers 174
Thomson Reuters 63-4
tick 166
time-weighted average price (TWAP) 166
top-tier prime brokers 86, 94
total return swap transaction (TRS) 30, 44-5, 46, 74,
    112
trade allocation methodologies 144, 145, 147
trade blotter 166
trade execution 31, 113-17
trade execution and capture (FX) 96
traded credit 112
trading desks 72, 104, 166
trading discretion 30
trading factors 41-51
trading platforms 36, 45-6
traditional asset managers 81-2, 175
tranched index trades 74, 77
tranches 166
transaction legs 117, 122, 125, 128, 160, 163

transaction size (securities) 113
transferable securities 56
transparency 174
transparent capital introduction process 35
tri-party agents 120
Triad Securities 10
trustee services 31

U

UBS 10, 59, 73
UCITS III 21, 54, 56
UK Listing Authority (UKLA) 59
uncollateralisation 125
Undertakings for Collective Investment in Transferable
    Securities see UCITS III
underwritings 72
universities 22
unmatched book 166
US Securities and Exchange Commission see SEC
US sub-prime crisis 57

V

value proposition 100-1
vanilla currency options 96
variable return securities 103
variation margin (securities) 114
verification notes 40
Vestima+ 65
volatility 15, 16
volume weighted average price (VWAP) 166

W

warrants 118
Warren Buffer buy-and-hold investment model 91
wealth management 72
websites 178
Wood, Jon 89

Other Titles in the Bizle Professional Series

Business Knowledge for IT
in Global Investment Banking

Business Knowledge for IT
in Trading and Exchanges

Business Knowledge for IT
in Private Equity

Business Knowledge for IT
in Insurance

Business Knowledge for IT
in Islamic Finance

Business Knowledge for IT
in Mobile Telecoms

These and other exciting titles can be pre-ordered from
Amazon sites worldwide or on www.essvale.com

Lightning Source UK Ltd.
Milton Keynes UK
23 November 2009

146619UK00001B/30/P